Repositioned Crowns

Presented by LaQuisha Hall
Coauthored by Couture'd Queens

Copyright © 2017 LaQuisha Hall

All rights reserved.

ISBN: 154329894X
ISBN-13: 978-1543298949

Dedication

To every woman who has had her crown slip and did not know how to adjust it... to the women who were never called or who never knew they were queens... this is for you.

Rise and reign.

Contents

	Acknowledgments	i
	Preface: Walk on Gold, Queens	2
1	Joy Comes in the Morning	5
2	What God Has for You: Don't Settle	15
3	Dear Queen	27
4	Rise and Reign	37
5	Run Me My Crown	48
6	Secrets	57
7	God's Confident Woman	65
8	Please Forgive Me	73
9	Reclaiming My Crown of Self-Worth	83
10	Breakthrough Bombshell	94
11	The Covering	101

12	Confessions of a Rejected Queen	107
13	Identity Theft	116
14	The Bottom	126
15	From Concrete to Crown	134
	About the Authors	142

Repositioned Crowns

Acknowledgements

Thank you to each coauthor for trusting LaQuisha Hall to support and walk you through the process of your first publication. Thank you to Mardis C. Hall for your assistance with this project. Thank you to the family, friends and community members who support each and every one of the queens included in this anthology.

Preface: Walk on Gold, Queens

I believe in telling your story. I have experienced the authority of the words *I am a survivor*. I have lived the life of conquering my fears and using what tried to hold me down to lift others up. I wanted other queens to experience the same. As a visionary and a creative, this is how Repositioned Crowns was birthed.

This is the only the beginning for each and every queen included. Their stories do not end with the words on these pages. They are reigning queens, leaders of many who will follow them. There are so many more for them to share their stories with, so many more books to be written, so much for them to do to exercise their authority overall.

Outside of sharing their truth and loving and

supporting each other through this process, each of these queens hold a special place in my heart. **Afia**, who is now a beautiful global leader was once a young teen in my mentoring program, Queendom T.E.A.; **Aisha**, a glamazon who fiercely walks many runways and shows up to assist me whenever I need her is a former SheRose Awards honoree; **Alexus**, one of my former scholars who has been to my home was also a young teen in my mentoring program, Queendom T.E.A.; **Charon**, my sister queen, confidante and laughing buddy who sends me happy mail; **Dawania**, a queen whose smile leaves an aroma of happiness wherever she goes and who always offers her support in any way whenever she sees me; **Eleshia**, who was never afraid to jump and will always ask for help; **Joi**, God's Confident Woman who reigns alongside me; **Keona**, the mother of my child and the Executive Director of my mentoring program who shows up all day every day for me; **LaKita**, who never sees it as a robbery to allow another queen to shine in her palace which makes her individual shine even brighter; **Mica**, a former scholar who always paid attention to me when I was her teacher and still does today; **Mone't**, who has become one of my closest friends and does not hesitate when I cry for help; **Shakira**, who enthusiastically keeps me in life as she so graciously walks the runway of life in sexy stillettos; **Shawan**, my fabulous soror and driven soldier for Christ, **Temica**, the Queen of Tenacity, who seems to never sleep due to all of the greatness she is constantly releasing into the world; and **Violesia**, who maintains a smile no matter what she is experiencing and looks fashionably chic while doing so.

Proud is an understatement... I am elated and

overjoyed to present these 15 queens who have repositioned their crowns... Showing up for others and themselves in supernatural ways. They are the real Wonder Women; they have the power to heal, set free and push the next queen on to her own throne. These queens embody my philosophy of *walking on gold*: Understanding that they were not born to be mediocre and that elevation was possible and even mandatory for them. They live the *Unbothered Queen* lifestyle: not allowing anyone or anything to keep them from their destined rise as Queens. But first, they had to release their own stories...

Queens, what an honor to assist you as you *Cue the Queen* within you!

LaQuisha Hall
Couture'd Confidence Coach
LaQuishaHall.com

Afia Yeboah

He is the God who avenges me, who subdues nations under me, who saves me from my enemies. You exalted me above my foes; from a violent man you rescued me. Therefore, I will praise you, Lord, among the nations; I will sing the praises of your name.

Psalm 18:47-49

It was the best day of my life! As a senior at Baltimore Polytechnic Institute, I had just received the most incredible news: I had been selected to be granted a full academic scholarship to the University of Maryland College Park! I was 1 of 18 total recipients in the entire city of Baltimore (with only one other winner from my school). I was chosen to be an Incentive Awards Program Recipient with full tuition awarded, room and board paid, and enriching community support offered for the next four years!

To have an opportunity to attend college, especially on a scholarship, was one of the single most life-changing things that could have ever happened to me. This gave me a greater capacity to be all I could be. A better shot at life.

Growing up in Baltimore was no walk in the park, but those who do survive are incredibly strong. I wasn't born with a silver spoon in my mouth—not even a plastic one. But in my mind I was "enriched" because I grew up in an inner city village with extended family and friends. My neighbors all looked out for one another. Even though it was considered to be "the ghetto", it was harmonious, I was always good in my hood, and collectively, we all coexisted well.

This scholarship, however, was my ticket out of an infamous city. I have had lifelong dreams of being an entertainment or corporate attorney. I commenced college undeclared. I tried my luck as a business major but failed that sophomore semester miserably. After prayer and self-reflection, I found my niche as an English major. Throughout my childhood, my mother called me her "Joy", and encouraged my love for reading and writing, so English was a perfect fit for me. I was a proud English major. I always enjoyed writing strong papers under strict deadlines. I was the friend that everyone would send their written work to for a peer review.

During college, I volunteered at soup kitchens,

homeless shelters and food banks to offer support to those in need. I also made school visits to numerous middle schools and high schools in my city. After years of making incredible memories and learning more about myself, I finally made it to my senior year. In order to meet the foreign language requirement needed to graduate, I had the opportunity to study abroad for the winter semester in Chile, South America. This would be my first international venture and I was so excited!

To say my semester abroad in Chile was a wonderful experience would be an understatement. My students were incredibly warm and joyful. Even at their tender elementary-school ages, they were extremely receptive to learning English. I spent recreational time with these Chilean students, accompanied them on cultural field trips, and volunteered further by beautifying their school. This was where I discovered international volunteer work was special, rewarding, and a great fit for me.

After the enriching experience of spending the winter semester of my senior year abroad, it was time to return home to complete my senior year and graduate in the spring! I submitted all of the required assignments for the winter semester in a timely fashion. My academic advisor informed me that all I needed was my final grade to be posted from my winter course in Chile to meet my credit requirements. This would deem me eligible for spring graduation. Without a doubt, I was counting down the days until I could walk across the stage and receive my diploma!

A week after reaching out to my Chilean instructor for my grade, much to my dismay, I received an email informing me that I had received a grade of an "I" for "Incomplete". I was requested to meet in the instructor's office to discuss the final paper that I had submitted. "What could be the issue?", I wondered. A few days later, I attended the meeting to find that my instructor had compared a highlighted portion of my paper to an article I cited. My instructor was accusing me of plagiarism.

Plagiarism is a dangerous accusation. It can be grounds for immediate dismissal from an academic institution and it permanently follows you on your transcript.

I was sick to my stomach. I could literally feel my world crashing down around me. Me? Committing plagiarism? No way. This was my senior year of college. I had never cheated on any assignment, I had never copied a quote without citing, and I took pride in all of my work.

While in tears and grossly offended at such a painful and false accusation, my instructor told me, " you will never be a lawyer if you keep being this dishonest".

I was hurt. After completing such fulfilling volunteer work and pouring my all into every paper I had ever written, to be accused of something so vile really hit me to the core. I was in shock. I assured her I had never been dishonest on any of my assignments and showed her where I had cited my source. I reiterated that I never cheated, that I had never committed plagiarism and that I never would. I offered to resubmit the assignment. I even offered to take a grade of "0" on the assignment, even though I knew I had done nothing wrong.

No. My instructor was fixated on accusing me of

plagiarism and thus, determined to get me kicked out of the University of Maryland for academic dishonesty.

It was the worst thing that could ever happen to me. It wasn't right, it wasn't fair, and it wasn't true. I was devastated. Shocked. Being at this great university meant the world to me. Having this chance to attend and graduate college was a once in a lifetime opportunity. And now, here stood before me a moment where it could all be robbed. All the hard work I poured into school – in vain, the four years of studying – wasted, and my integrity – questioned and under scrutiny.

At the time that I was accused of plagiarism, I felt a series of different emotions. First, I was just afraid: I was scared that all of the hard work I had accomplished would be in vain. How would people look at me now? As dishonest? As a cheater? Then, I was offended: I couldn't believe that after all this time in my honest academic career, someone would have the audacity to accuse me of something so unethical. After reaffirming myself, and reminding myself that I was not guilty, I was determined to advocate for myself and prove myself right: that I was not a cheater, that I was not a liar, and that I did not plagiarize. At this crucial point in my life, I turned to God as my rock, and every day I would pray to be vindicated. I got closer to God than I ever had been, joined a local church nearby and read the book of Psalms every day.

In the weeks to come, I was seen before the Office of Student Conduct. I decided to do a self-referral, and I took the paper accused of plagiarism to this Office to be reviewed.

After careful review and their discussion with my accusing professor, the final decision was that I was found **not guilty** of plagiarism, but that I would, however, receive a grade of zero (0) on the paper assignment for the course, at the request of my professor. In addition to receiving a grade of zero on the assignment, I was required to successfully complete an Academic Integrity Seminar online. The seminar required that I reflect upon my personal values and academic integrity. This whole process made me discover my inner strength and fortitude: though I may bend, I will never break.

The case was closed! I was so relieved that I was indeed found not guilty of plagiarism!

When it was over, all I could do was praise God that I was proven innocent. I was excited to graduate, and I vowed to always write with purpose and direction, in a way that could never again be questioned.

This trial all unfolded during my final semester college. I was taking 17 credits in a total of 7 classes, and I graduated with straight A's. Now that I look back on it all, I see that God used this trial as my testimony. This was one of the best things that ever happened to me because it helped me tap into a power that I didn't even know I had. I learned how powerful it was to pray and to let God fight your battles. My family and the academic community at Maryland who knew and loved me showed me incredible support in such a trying time. My dear aunt proclaimed, "they tried to run you over with a bus but they didn't know you would become the bus driver!"

Never in my life have I been so close to God. Today I have a nonstop, open dialogue, where I tell Him everything. And when I say everything, I mean whatever comes across my mind, if I feel an urge to run it by Him, I address it to Him. I invite the Holy Spirit to enter into the situation at hand, and I put it all in God's hands.

At graduation, I was awarded the Sara Ann Soper Service Award for the English major that had the most exemplary community service locally and abroad.

As I was walking off stage, to my surprise, the very same instructor who accused me of plagiarism 90 days prior to this day was in attendance, clapping and congratulating me.

In that moment, I thought to myself, "Wow, maybe even she knew within her own spirit that I was innocent." I assumed that her attendance was what she needed to come to peace with herself on such a gross accusation.

I was so happy, beaming with joy, that not only I was proven innocent, but also that I was graduating with honor. My name is now even displayed on the wall in the English Department, with all of the other Sara Ann Soper Service Award recipients who came before me. I knew with faith that only God could turn a situation like this around so righteously. I trusted that it wasn't my own doing but that the entire time God had been working on my behalf.

I knew from here on out, that if any trials of life were to present themselves, I knew to trust in God that I would come out on top, so no longer would I shake. I now believed I could be steadfast and know that God was and always would be working things out for me. And I am so grateful that He is.

After graduation, I started work at an intellectual property law firm which was an incredible experience that further developed my interest in international affairs. The summer after graduating from college, I studied for the LSAT for three months. However, something didn't feel right. I had been working at this incredible law firm, yet law did not bring me the conviction that I thought I should have. By the time registration for the LSAT rolled around, I could not bring myself to register.

My instructor may not have been totally wrong. No, I was not dishonest, but was there a chance that law may not have been for me after all?

Then these magic words presented themselves to me: *Afia, how will you make a difference? What mark will you make on this world?*

We often say, "I don't know what I want. I have no idea what I want to do." However, I don't think that is true. I actually think, more often than not, we know EXACTLY what it is we want to do. But we are simply afraid. Afraid of success or afraid of failure, and oftentimes, fear simply paralyzes us. So I answered my own question: I wanted to make a global change. I decided my first stop would be China.

I moved on to the most beautiful volunteer experience in Beijing, China. My time spent in Beijing was incredible. I was able to work directly with four children and I helped them further develop their English reading and writing skills. I couldn't believe it: this little Black girl from Baltimore was making her mark on the world again in another international experience. In my free time, I spent time exploring Beijing, and visiting amazing sites, including one of the seven wonders of the world: The Great Wall of China. I was also able to see the venue where the 2008 Beijing Olympics were held: the Beijing National Stadium.

After this experience, I returned home and finished up my Teaching English as a Foreign Language certification. Thanks to the support of my family and favor from God, just several months after my time in China, I went on to my next international venture in Colombia, South America. I spent 5 months in Colombia, completing over 400 hours of service. Colombia was incredible too. I was apart of a great initiative to enrich the lives of others by helping children further develop their English language skills.

Most recently, I participated in the Greenheart Global Leaders Conference in D.C., where I had the honor and privilege to speak before the Department of State, advocating for communities in need such as Baltimore and cities that are like it, domestically and abroad. In my speech to the State Department, I stated, "Transforming our world is no easy feat, but it can be done. It starts with you and me. It starts when we draw from something deeper within ourselves to care about others. It's when you care about the health and well being of your neighbors, just as much as you do about those who you may never even meet. I am determined to bring about positive changes to my city and cities around the world. I will be continuously investing in and contributing to inclusiveness, safety, resiliency and sustainability, as often as I can and in as many ways and places that I can, nationwide and globally."

I followed my heart and made my dreams come true. I have committed to creating positive change internationally, and in the inner city that I was raised in and taught me the value of social activism: Baltimore City, Maryland, USA.

I've traveled alone, internationally, at ages 21, at 22, and at 23, which is what some consider tender ages. People have often told me, "Afia, you're so fearless". However this is simply not true. What I learned is that in life is that **sometimes you must suspend fear in order to make things happen for yourself.**

The students that I have worked with at home and abroad all have an incredible need: to be invested in, to have opportunity afforded to them, and to be adequately represented. I dream that students from impoverished backgrounds from all over the world are not counted out, but instead, have a real chance at engaging with the rest of the world. As for my future, I will continue to make an impact, locally and internationally, as often as possible. I will spend the rest of my life in the service of others, because that is what I truly love to do. The rest is in God's hands.

You've got this. Be blessed, be brilliant, be grateful, own your life and love yourself! You can't be stopped!

What God Has for You: Don't Settle

Aisha Watson

But as it is written, Eye has not seen, nor ear heard, neither have entered into the heart of man, the things which God has prepared for them that love him.

1 Corinthians 2:9

Have you ever written a letter to the Universe? I mean, like sit down with a pen and piece of paper and tell the universe exactly what you want and/or desire? Well, I did. Almost a year ago, along with a few friends, who were all fed up with the type of men that were coming into our lives, we all decided to write the universe a letter, outlining exactly what we wanted in our mate. (or at lease what we thought we wanted). So one night, in the back of my notebook, I wrote to the universe *everything* I wanted in a mate.

    I realized one morning while washing the dishes that the universe delivered. Although I was being as specific as I could be at the time, what the universe delivered this time around, wasn't what I was looking for at that point in my life. Don't get me wrong, he was tall, cooked good meals, had his own house and car, a stable job and a sense of humor, but there was absolutely no chemistry. Was I being too picky? Nah. I just refused to settle. I had to look myself in the eye and be honest with myself. Would this be a compromise that I could live with? In the end it would not be. I let him down gently and walked away.

Don't Settle

    Now, since healing from my past, I learned to wholeheartedly love myself. I treated myself to spa days quarterly; I even saved up to be able to treat myself to some new shoes or a vintage purse from time to time. What I'm saying, is that you have to pamper and prepare yourself for your king. Just as he is out there being prepared for you. Knowing your worth will allow you to recognize and sort through mess that doesn't belong in your life. You knew he was too young, but you went along with it anyway. You knew he couldn't hold a job down consistently but you stayed anyway. Queens don't settle; we rule!

As my grandmother would say, "Potential doesn't pay the bills." So why settle for it?

There is seldom any lasting fulfillment in settling. It's unfortunate how our minds allow us to rationalize situations. I agree that there is some compromising when it comes to lasting relationships, but compromising your Queendom is not an option. Stop rationalizing and start realizing that you are in fact a queen.

I saw a meme the other day that stated, "We all eat lies when we are hungry". Stop being so hungry for a relationship that you end up in a situation where you are miserable! We've all been there at some point. Heck! I birthed a child for him, married him and was simply miserable. When I woke up (literally), the lies he was feeding me no longer worked. I made up my mind and began to see that I deserved more. The grasp he had on me for most of my twenties had come to an abrupt end.

Let Go

I learned through various situations to live by faith, not by feelings. My feelings would have caused me to continue in the downward spiral that I was mentally trapped in. My faith showed me that God was my true provider and He has been ever since.

Living by faith and not by feelings, can save your life, mentally, physically and spiritually. The closer you get to God, the more you can see how wonderfully and fabulously made you are. Stop doubting yourself, for if he brings to you to it, He'll bring you through it! For I survived a physically and mentally abusive marriage, and my son who was labeled as mentally handicapped in Elementary school successfully graduated from high school. In all that I've been through, God continues to shape and mold me for his purpose. Thus preparing me for greater. That greater may come in the form of a mate, a ministry, a job. Nonetheless, what God has for me is for me. The same applies to you.

You can still walk in your greatness even if you need to wear a shirt sating "Beware: Damaged Goods." Allow me to explain: I used this term to describe myself recently in the hair salon and it upset another young lady nearby. I asked her if when she went to a supermarket would she purchase an item in which the can was banged up or the box torn and tapped back together. She scrunched up her face and said no. I told her to think of that in a reverse sense. People often look at the outside, not realizing that the goods have been damaged from negative life experiences, however the contents of the box or can are usually perfectly fine and would taste the same.

I don't use the term as a way to lower my worth as that marked down, dented can in the supermarket. I use it as a way of recognizing the work that I am continually doing as I grow into a more confident and spiritually polished self. This growth can only take place when you recognize the unhealthy relationships and habits in your life and make a plan to overcome them. This plan can come in many forms including but not limited to reading scriptures for guidance, counseling from a professional (girlfriends can be biased), meditation, Pilates and/or yoga to gain peace. Regardless of the strategy to get your crown straightened, after making the realization, the next step is cleaning house and letting go.

What is it that you need to let go of so God can continue to work on you? Not everyone or everything in your life is meant for what God has in store for you. Your blessings are on the other side of letting go. Let go of what doesn't help you to grow. Pull up those weeds so the fruits of your labor can blossom through!

Create the Vision

I currently have four vision boards that have helped me during my journey. Two are motivational and the other two outline things that I look forward to in life, like my convertible, my extra-long tub (if you've seen me in person, you'll get it), my wedding dress, and my future engagement ring. For it's said, what you visualize, materializes! Once you train your mind for greatness, you will be less likely to settle for something or someone who doesn't fit into that vision.

Overcoming the Damaged Goods Syndrome

I label the "Beware: Damaged Goods" as a syndrome because there is a mindset that consumes those who have been in unhealthy relationships at any point in their lives. Once recognized, one must muster the will and motivation to heal and become whole. When I really sat down and analyzed how I ended up in a mentally and physically abusive relationship, I had to do some serious soul searching. It's wasn't so much blaming myself, but it was a process in identifying, what in my past was damaged and clouding my judgment.

I was raised in a loving household by both parents. As the oldest I was held at a pretty high standard, and did my best to walk a straight line. My parents did a great job at keeping my two younger siblings and I pretty busy. I was in dance school since the age of three, had my first assistant camp counselor job at 12. Academically I was on the honor roll and received the citizenship award pretty frequently. I was even in the church choir, where I served as the Regional Parish Representative.

So how in the world did I end up in a relationship fearing for my life? That's the million dollar question. It wasn't until my first year of college that a professor embarrassed me by informing me in front of a class of peers, just how sheltered my upbringing was. Me? Sheltered? How insulting. At the time I was devastated, but later realized that factor would later play a role in my future.

Another factor was my father. Don't get me wrong, he loved us dearly and was an outstanding provider. He worked every day and even did overtime when it was available. I wouldn't consider myself a daddy's girl. Although I was the first born, my youngest sister took that role hands down. I have wonderful childhood memories of family vacations, snowball fights, Mrs. Pac-Man PlayStation tournaments and even a time when he hit his head on the doorway as he jumped into the room trying to frighten us. What I don't remember is my father being present at any of my dance recitals. They took place annually from age three to 17. I have no memory of him being there. Not once.

This is where my damage began. I grew up never knowing if I was good enough in my father's eyes.

Unfortunately, it wasn't until adulthood that I realized how this was affecting the choices I'd made in relationships. I had a pattern of settling for mates who had a great work ethic but were weak in making me feel secure or even wanted in the relationship. They conducted themselves in ways where I felt less than appreciated, but yet I stayed. I was tormented by a rollercoaster of emotions due to the unhealthiness of the relationships.

I met my ex-husband at a concert put on by a local radio station. He sat in the row in front of me and was eyeballing my dancer's body covered in a TLC half top. I just knew I was cute. We exchanged numbers by the end of the night and began dating not long after. He was the manager at a fast food restaurant so I just knew I'd hit the jackpot. He took me on trips to various states and spoiled me with affection. That's until he began drinking with friends. When he drank he became loud and physically aggressive towards me. I brushed it off thinking he was showing off for his friends, so that younger me tolerated it.

His drinking and aggression got him into trouble with the law. He was incarcerated while I was five months pregnant with our child. Two months prior his drinking influenced the first time he beat me to the point that I didn't leave our apartment for days. It was New Year's Eve. I was in my last year of college and needed a way out. I thought him being incarcerated was my opportunity to escape.

I gave birth to our child in August and moved to Maryland after completing my Bachelor's degree. One of the hardest decisions was leaving my child with my mother for five weeks until I was settled and had enough money to be able to provide for him. By that spring, his father was out of jail and made plans to move to Maryland. He wrote love letters to me weekly and a part of me believed that he had changed. By the summer of 2000, I leased a townhouse and he moved in shortly afterwards.

All was going ok for some time and he even proposed. We had a gorgeous wedding in Montego Bay, Jamaica in the presence of my mother and sister. My father did not attend, a factor I should have taken into account as a warning sign. We were in marital bliss until we returned home. Within a week he lost his job and his drinking increased heavily. I was working at a school, doing home schooling and teaching dance classes in order for us to stay afloat. Yet none of my efforts were accepted in his eyes. The abuse started verbally and increased to shoving me against the wall to pushing down the steps. Our toddler son was present for these moments and I feared the echoes of my screams reverberating in his head.

The police were called to our townhome so much that they knew his name and his car. I was embarrassed, especially since I worked in the local school system. I attempted to run and escape his torment on numerous occasions, but he always found my son and I and dragged us back. I got to the point where I was mentally and physically tired. Over the years of the relationship he had found a way to separate me from my friends and family. He tried to make it so that only he and our child existed in our little world. Helpless is not a strong enough term to describe the anguish and pain I endured.

The last time he put his hands on me was the

first time that I fought back. The cops were called once again. This time I pressed charges and got an ex parte' so he would be removed from the home. Due to the type of charges I was referred the Sexual Assault/Spouse Abuse Resource Center (SARC) for counseling. I was hesitant but knew I needed something because even with the ex parte' in place he still harassed me through phone calls and letters.

Through my counseling I learned the different types of abuse. Until this time, I had not realized that I was being verbally and emotionally abused for years. For me, these are the bruises that have seemed to last much longer and are more difficult to heal from.

I stayed in counseling for months, participating in groups and individual sessions. Eventually my then husband continued breaking into the home and finding other ways back into our lives. He lied to the police saying I had let him back in thus making the ex parte' null and void. Once again I was helpless. I continued counseling and worked on improving myself. I even tried to get him to go to marriage counseling with me. At some point I had set my mind on not becoming a statistic. I wholeheartedly wanted my marriage to work. Plus, wasn't it a sin to get a divorce? That was my mindset. The fear of being a failure in my marriage superseded the abuse I was enduring. I later realized this stemmed from the inferior mindset of not being good enough for my father.

My father strongly disliked my husband. Better yet, he hated him. Thus, he refused to attend the destination wedding. To this day I still am perplexed as to why he didn't sit me down and talk me out of it. My mother did her best to support me in any way she could, but she stepped back after my ex-husband put her out of the house during an argument. After that incident I really had no one. I continued counseling and even joined a local church and one of its arts ministries. That became my new outlet. The word of God. I began to see that God had not created man to suffer, nor did he create me to continue suffering in an unhealthy marriage.

Time passed and we were three months from having to renew our lease on the townhome. And just like that I woke up. I mean literally. One day I woke up, looked at my husband and informed him that I didn't know him anymore. Quietly I began looking for two bedroom apartments for my son and I. Within two months, I found a place and was approved to move in. With the help of some of my coworkers, I moved out and never turned back. I want to tell you that I felt like Super Woman and just started over without blinking an eye. Nope. I was an emotional wreck! I doubted my ability to provide for my son and myself. I beat myself up for becoming a single mom. I remembered my mother being at the apartment while unpacking. She walked over to me, held my face in her hands and said, "Aisha, stop crying about being a single mother, for although he was physically there, you already were". This was such an eye opener for me! I paid the rent, childcare, food electric etc., etc.! It wasn't the first time, nor would it be the last, and she was definitely accurate. Even while married I was a single mother. From that point on I worked hard to make sure my son was provided for.

I wish I could say that after I left him it was like the movies and all went dark and quiet. Not hardly.

He continued to call me daily, even tried to commit suicide twice. The second time I told him to hang up and call 911. I was mentally done! I had enough of him draining all of my positive energy. My father raised me as a queen. He consistently told us that our ancestors are royalty. So why in the world was I responding like I was less? How did I allow another human being to dehumanize me to the point that my crown had slid from its rightful place?

I have to confess that it took years to heal from that brokenness and parts of my heart are still in the "Damaged Goods" section. But I praise God daily for how far I've come. Sometimes people think I'm joking when I say that I am so glad I don't look like what I've been through! Hallelujah! Ever since putting my life in God's hands my walk is different! My wardrobe is different! My vocabulary is different! My crown has been repositioned and it was nothing but the grace of God which brought me through!

If you are reading this and you've found yourself in a dark place not knowing where to turn, turn to the Lord! Remember to live by faith, not by feelings! Feelings will get you bound up in a mess. Faith will free you from that bondage. I am a true testament that through Christ, I can do all things! Believe that you can make it! Believe that God will bring you through! Believe that God has given you the tools to survive whatever situation you may feel trapped in. Whether it's an unhealthy relationship, a stressful job, a child that just can't get their life together! Give it over to God and believe what His word says. Find comfort in Jesus! My mentor once told me, the only time you take off your crown is to polish it. So reposition your crown and take your rightful throne in grace!

Proverbs 3:5 says to *trust in the Lord with all your heart, and do not lean on your own understanding.*

Alexus Hobbs

Now you understand just why my head's not bowed.
I don't shout or jump about or have to talk real loud.
When you see me passing it ought to make you proud.
I say, It's in the click of my heels,
The bend of my hair, the palm of my hand,
The need of my care,'
Cause I'm woman Phenomenally.
Phenomenal woman, that's me!

"Phenomenal Woman" by Maya Angelou

Dear Queen,

I hope that since my letter has reached you that you are filled with motivation, joy and drive. I pray to God that I am able to keep this experience going for you. Do you know that you are beautiful?. You are a strong queen and can overcome all the trials that you will endure.

Have you ever felt like you were not given a fair chance on the opportunities that everyone else was given? Being raised in a single parent home made me feeling like I was in a race that I would never win. Even though I felt this way when I was younger I learned that this experience taught me hard work and perseverance. We didn't always have what we wanted but we always had everything we needed.

High school was one of the most difficult times in my life. My depression was very high and my confidence was very low. I didn't know my self-worth and the stress of being a teenager didn't help me stay sane. I was at the age of being heavily influenced by peer pressure and boys. I started to look for boys to validate my self-worth, until I met my high school English teacher, Mrs. Hall.

Mrs. Hall was so beautiful and she had the biggest and brightest smile I had ever seen. She greeted all her students with a motherly embrace and was so filled with love. I always felt a general desire to help others, yet I didn't know at the time the role Mrs. Hall would play in allowing this to come to pass. I appreciated Mrs. Hall's presence as she introduced me to her etiquette and mentoring program for young ladies, Queendom T.E.A. (The Etiquette Academy).

I admit that I didn't know what to expect

when I joined Queendom T.E.A , but I was excited to be a part of the program. Queendom eventually became my safe haven. I was able to express myself with a group of females I didn't know and having that opportunity made me more comfortable in my own skin. That same group of young women would later become my sisters. We built a bond with one another in Queendom. We held each other responsible for the next young lady because we were held to a high standard.

During this time every one of us (the queens) were fighting at least one battle, yet hoping for better days. I didn't know the importance of self love until I met Mrs. Hall. She embedded in us the fact that we were beautiful queens. She taught us that being a queen isn't just claiming the title but it is within your actions. We were also taught the importance of uplifting one another. One of my favorite memories from Queendom was the vent circles we had. We never knew how many battles we were fighting but when it was all released into the vent circle we realized we were all going through similar situations. I also loved the workshops we had. The workshops featured guest speakers, entrepreneurs and women of different backgrounds who had great success in their fields. These women would bring books they had written and allow us to participate in activities dealing with arts and crafts. Queendom guided us in dealing with life as young women. I took so much meaningful information away from this group of females. Even though I was so enlightened I still had insecurities that only I could face.

I met a guy, Kevin. We found one another on an online dating website. We talked on the phone for a few days. Once we realized we only lived a few minutes away from each other, we ended up meeting and it seemed to be love at first sight; we were inseparable. It was my first real relationship and he was older than me. He even gave me a ring! I thought he was the love of my life but when I caught on to his infidelity it broke my heart. I cried for three nights straight and practically starved. That was my first taste of heart break and it felt so bad. He cheated on me with a girl he only knew from Facebook. It took me so long to heal from the pain he caused.

    I went into a downward spiral afterwards. I acted out against my mom, ran away from home and stayed out late--I completely lost myself. I was in so much pain and didn't understand how to cope with it. I ended up going to therapy. I was so against the idea of expressing how I felt but I didn't realize how much I was hurting myself. Eventually everything came to a halt. My negativity started to catch up with me. I was so unhappy on the inside but no one knew until I tried hurting myself. When I finally let someone know it was a relief but I had to go to a psychiatric ward for a mental evaluation. I spent a week there and it was well needed. I had time and space to process my decisions. My mom was there the whole time. Before the hospitalization, I knew my mom loved me but I had put her through so much hurt and pain that I was not sure if she still loved me. However, I felt an obligation to make her proud of me.

    Being released was one of the happiest times of my life. I felt like I had a clean slate and I didn't want to mess that up. I used my coping skills for a very long time but I still wasn't as happy. I was so focused on pleasing others and gaining my mom's trust back that I was never satisfied. I remembered Mrs. Hall words on self-love which allowed me to forgive the old me and move on from the mistakes of my past. Eventually things started to come together.

In 2012, I graduated from high school with the 2nd highest GPA and I was the first person in my generation to finish--another one of the happiest moments of my life. Immediately after high school I started culinary school. My first year was bitter sweet and I started to see a pattern that I allowed to continue. My next few years in culinary school was up and down and I didn't have a job. Not being able to do things I wanted to do because I was broke gave me an arresting feeling but I kept my faith because I knew better days were coming. In March 2014, I got my first job in a kitchen! I felt like my luck was turning around and I worked so much but it kept me positively occupied. It felt like I had purpose and I was progressing.

Kevin would peek in and out of my life asking for forgiveness but I wasn't willing to let go of the pain he caused. Deep down inside I missed him so much. I wished I could have just forgiven him. I loved him so much but the hurt was so deep. Working at my new job was a dream come true but it was nothing school could prepare me for. I love the rush, the crazy hours and the food. It made me happy feeding others, witnessing their facial expressions of satisfaction. A year after being there I got another job in the food industry. It was an overnight job and I survived the first 6 months but eventually I became tired. I would work both jobs for another 6 months before I stopped. Working so much made me leave school and I started to lose my dream. I wanted to succeed so bad but I lost myself in the mist of it. I decided to stop and get myself together at the time and I only had a few classes until I was done. I couldn't quit but I needed to step back.

My next move would be moving into my own apartment. I had known for a very long time it was time for me to spread my wings. In February 2016 I was offered a job at a well-known hospital. Also during this time, I found an apartment. All the pieces were coming together. I didn't have to work at my old job because my new job would cover my bills and expenses when I moved into my new place. I watched my dreams unfold in front of me and on top of all this good news, I went back to school. It wasn't easy but I made it. I felt so spiritually lifted.

In the mist of all my blessings I ran into Kevin, again. He begged me to give him a chance to make it up to me. He sold me on the idea of us becoming a power couple. I was so vulnerable at this point because I thought the last piece in my puzzle would be a knight in shining armor. Somehow he made me believe that this knight was him. I thought he changed as he showed me a new him and we eventually ended up moving in together. It was a fast move, but he was homeless at the time; as his girlfriend, I felt like it was my obligation to make sure he was safe. I kept the news of him moving in to myself because I knew it was so fast but it eventually got out.

We had an awesome first few months. I still had doubts but these feelings slowly went away. We split the bills which allowed us to have extra money. We had date nights and above all he showed me off as his Queen. Up to that point in my life I felt like nothing could go wrong. I had a guy that loved and adored me, I had a good paying job, I had my own place and I was almost done with school. But, this eventually came to an end.

I wanted more out of life I wasn't done knocking my goals down. He didn't have the same dreams I did. I would hear him reminisce about the old days when he had cars and a good paying job. I would soon become fed up with the stories and wanted to make a reality of it. My goal wasn't about money, it was about happiness and freedom to roam the world and all its beauty; he didn't have that same spark. Money issues surfaced and that divided us more. I wanted our next step to be a car and he wasn't as persistent as I was. I felt like the extra money left over after paying bills should be saved towards a car. He wasn't comfortable with giving me money unless he knew for sure it was for the bills. Our relationship started to fall apart even more when he began to flirt with girls on the internet--the same reason we broke up the first time. However, the difference from then and now was he began to destroy our home.

One time we had a disagreement and we didn't talk for the rest of the day. It was close to bed time and he thought I was ignoring him, so he threw his phone so hard against the floor it shattered into pieces. I woke up screaming and he embraced me with his arms apologizing, telling me he was sorry. He told me he couldn't handle me ignoring him. That night I didn't get much sleep. From that moment on I didn't get any good sleep. Kevin had more outbursts that I swept under the rug and shrugged off to him just being angry. The last day that I would see was coming.

    The day before Kevin and I took my sisters for a girl's day out, we got dinner, manicures and pedicures. We had such an awesome time but towards the end of the night the atmosphere changed. The guy I was paying to give us a ride home showed up late. Kevin already didn't like him because he thought the guy liked me. We dropped my sisters off at their home and had to rush to get our things out of my mom's house. He asked me if we had the phone he was trying to fix and I assured him we did. We finally made it home. I ran to the bathroom while Kevin began to look for the phone. He couldn't find the phone so he began to become angry. He assumed I left it at my mom's house so we started to argue. I was still in the bathroom and our argument became heated. He started to irritate me so I told him to leave me alone which made him even angrier. As we exchanged words back forth he started to mess the house up. He came in the bathroom and ripped the shower curtains off the hooks and threw everything around. I became angry; the disrespect was enough. I was tired of being scared of living with him so I told him to leave. He grabbed my phone and threw it against the wall but it didn't break. We started to fight over the phone and he got a hold of it and threw it against the window which made it shatter.

    I told started yelling, "Why do you keep breaking our things? Why are you destroying our home?"

    Angry, Kevin started to pace. I kept yelling for him to get out. It seemed to trigger him as he began to drag me and push me up against the wall, but I fought back, punching and screaming. He began to get the best of me and dragged me into our bedroom where he repeatedly hit me in my face and head. I begged for him to stop. He grabbed my face and bit it. I felt my soul leave my body I was in so much pain.

As I burst out in tears he started to panic and say, "I can't go back to jail!"

Kevin grabbed a knife and held it up to me. I promised him I wasn't going to send him to jail. I had to reassure him that we would work through it all. In the back of my head I knew I couldn't live like this but I'd rather pretend to live like that to save my life. We began to clean everything up and he started to become calm. He was still a little edgy but we could talk about it. He needed to go to the store but before he left he said he saw my brothers and uncles outside; he smirked, then left. He returned back monitoring me and looking at my face. Once we finally got settled in we laid down and he watched me. I pretended to fall asleep and slept very lightly, crying myself to sleep.

At that point, I thought about everything I learned in Queendom. I thought about Mrs. Hall and the words she used to describe someone like me: strong, beautiful, resilient, survivor. I was a queen, whether he knew it or not; I did.

The next day came and Kevin wouldn't let me leave. The only way I convinced him let me go was saying I had school. I packed my school bag like a regular day and left out. I ran to my mom's house and he texted me, asking me if that was that the last time I would see him. I never answered back.

A few days later, I got a restraining order against him. I cried myself to sleep for nights wondering why he did this to me. Why someone would want to kill me? My life flashed before my eyes. I thought about all the good and bad I had done and wondered if it was karma coming back to pay me a visit. I didn't realize how damaging he was to me. Emotional and physical abuse was there I just didn't want to see it. I didn't know if I would survive this storm. For the most part, I was a strong woman but never in a millions years I could see myself allowing someone to bring me so much hurt. As I look back at those events that lead up to this tragedy I knew I was better than that... I am a Queen and I deserved so much more.

Queen, this letter is not to persuade you to not be in a relationship. I just want you to be selfish with your love until someone proves they deserve it. I want you to be strong enough to know when its time to let go and when enough is enough. Above all, I want you to love yourself because that's where love starts.

Sincerely ,

A Repositioned Queen

Charon Richardson

I started living and not just walking around in misery. I started loving me and living in my authentic truth. I got out of my own way to allow me to shine!

The fear I felt was indescribable. I had to make that call. I had to tell her. She would find out soon. It was now or never. I put the quarter inside the pay phone. My heart was beating fast; I thought it will surely bounce out my chest. OMG, its ringing…

Our lives changed forever that day. I was scared, sixteen and pregnant. I was disappointed with myself; I was now a statistic, a black, teenager mother! My mom said "God doesn't make mistakes. There is a reason for everything He does." Her words didn't help. They didn't make me feel better; I was still disappointed and hated myself. What will I do with my life? How would I feed this child? Truth be told I never thought about being a mom, actually didn't think I would be a good one. Little did I know then, that my baby would save my life and lead me to my destiny.

The next months were so hard. I was ridiculed by most, shamed by the elders in my family and church. They said I ruined my life and disgraced my family, that I would NEVER amount to anything. My friends stop talking to me and talked about me, so I stopped going to school. I didn't want to be one of those girls that people pointed and gazed at when I walked by in the halls in my custom uniform for my growing belly. I remember my mom telling some "I will not throw my child in the streets". Everyone had their 20 cents to add to my life. I was scared; no one ever asked me what I wanted, how I felt or what I needed. I guess I gave up that right when (according to them) I destroyed my wonderful life. I'm not sure if it's an island thing or a generational thing but the worst situation you could get yourself into in an island home is to come home pregnant. It seemed like if I robbed a bank they wouldn't have anything to say. I realized then that I was on my own.

I didn't want to know the sex of the baby, but everyone would say you are having a boy as I had a small belly (again, adding their 20 cents). I did want a boy because I thought it would be easier. God in His wisdom knew better. On March 1988 I gave birth to a bouncing healthy 5 lb baby girl. Something changed and clicked inside of me. I knew instinctively that I had to be all I could be for her. I wanted her to be proud of me. I wanted her to look to me as her mentor. She didn't ruin my life… She saved me!

My mom was the best as she always had my back. I must admit I was lost for a really long time, trying to figure out what my purpose was on this earth. She supported my dream and she still does. She told me a billion times I could do anything I wanted to with God by my side. Even though I had the support, I didn't know what I wanted to be when I grew up. I was thrust into motherhood, into being an adult. People expected me to act as such, but the reality was I was a 16 year old, scared mother. Watching those almond shaped, big eyes of my baby made me not give up looking for what made me the happiest at my core.

I finished high school. YES, I DID! I did it! It wasn't easy, but it's what I had to do. The essence of me wouldn't let me rest until I was walking towards my destiny. There was this yearning, this fire for more. This was way before all these self-help books and shows talking about how to get to your destiny, how to find your God given talent. I just knew that where I was, wasn't my bliss, I was created for more and that I had to jump off the bridge (of life), and out of my comfort zone to become me, not for me but for my daughter.

I thank God for a praying Mother, who didn't give up on me. She believed in me when I didn't believe in myself. Mom was right "God doesn't make mistakes."

I remember the day that my destiny called me and I knew that it was time to leave St. Croix. In April 1996, my life changed. I moved to NYC to pursue my new found dream of becoming a world renowned Fashion Designer. It was so scary. I cried all the way from St. Croix to Puerto Rico, which was a 35 min plane ride. I was scared and fear overtook me but I didn't allow it to win. Leaving my daughter was one of the hardest things that I have had to do but it had to be done--- in order for me to be all that I could be so that she could be all she needed to be. I had to make that jump… I had to fly with fear!

Four years flew by so fast. I graduated with honors from the Fashion Institute of Technology College in NYC. This world renowned college had classes taught by some of the world greatest designers. Students come from all over the world came to attend. I did it, again! I had broken the cycle and proved everyone wrong. I was smart. I was not going to be living on public assistance I would not depend on my parents and I would be a great mom.

As the oldest of 5 girls, I was my mother's first child to graduate from college. I was the same daughter that came home pregnant at 15, delivering at 16. It was such an honor for me to watch her watch me get my degree. My heart was full that day. There is no greater feeling as a parent to see your kids succeed and become everything that you wish for them in their lives. I'm honored that I can give that gift to my parents. The greatest part was that my daughter was also watching me make those steps across the stage to receive my degree.

The Shift

I can't believe this! I'm just an island *gyal* who had a dream. Was this really happening? Was I really going there? I have only been a designer for 3 years and someone believes in me this much. I was filled with various emotions; fear and joy ripple threw me. Twenty hours later, I landed in Hong Kong.

I remember the first time that I went on a double decker plane heading towards Hong Kong. I was sitting in first class having champagne poured for me at a snap of a my finger. My job was to go to the factors in China and check on production of garments that would go to various stores like Macy's, Bloomingdales', Wal-Mart and Sears, just to name a few.

Have you heard that old wives tale that you can't buy happiness? I couldn't buy happiness but what I could buy was wine and more wine. I would drink myself to sleep every night at about two bottles or so, which helped shut my brain off. I did not love myself; I didn't even know who I was, or even what I needed. I was angry at the world. I was angry at myself that I was in an abusive relationship, that I had allowed somebody to take advantage of me. I was still mad at my 15-year-old Charon for getting pregnant and messing up her whole life. Hell, I was just mad at life, walking around with a chip on my shoulder. I was hurt and hurting everyone in my path. My dream was to become the Vice President of Design for a huge fashion house, but God had other plans.

There was a knock at my office door, "Hey Charon, can I come in?" asked Rebecca from the Human Resources Department.

"Of course," I replied. She closed the door as she came in the room. I was thinking that this conversation must be serious.

"Word just came... they will be closing a few departments and yours is one of them. Just wanted to give you a heads up."

"When?" I asked.

"After your Korea, Taiwan, China Trip."

I squealed in delight, "Awesome!" She look at me with disbelief that I was happy.

The truth was that I had the perfect job. I was the Design Director over a few brands. I traveled various times a year for fabric & trend research, as well as visited factories in numerous parts of Asia, but

I wasn't happy! I got up daily, went to work and sat in tons of meetings, and I still was not happy. I was well on my way to potentially becoming VP of Design but I wasn't happy in the core of me. I did my job exceptionally well; it was like breathing for me. I knew I should be happy because I dreamt of this... I worked hard for this... but the fact remained: I was not happy.

    I took a summer off to travel and relax beach side, trying to figure out what my next move was. Was I going to change careers? I use to love what I did, what happened? I fought to be a designer. I fought for the corner office. Against all odds, I DID IT! One day I went down to the basement and found my sewing supplies. I hadn't sewn since 2000, which was almost a decade ago. I dusted off my sewing machine and something marvelous ignited inside of me: joy! It was the feeling I got when I first learned to sew. I remembered sewing every single day for one month or so, all day long. I was blissfully happy. I created a whole new wardrobe for myself. I even started a sewing studio and started teaching sewing. I was utterly elated, but something was missing. I had no idea what or how to fix it.

    After a year and a half of chasing my happy, I was ready to go back to work force on my terms. Reality had set in. I had a daughter in college, mortgage and all that other "adult" stuff that I was responsible for. I was frustrated after about three months of job hunting and no call backs.

I shared this with my mom one day. She replied, "Why don't you ask God what he wants for you? You have never had to look hard for a job, they found you. Maybe it is time for a shift."

I was so confused. What does she mean what He wants for me? I wanted to go back to corporate work and travel the world on my terms. That was what I wanted; what was so hard about that?

I struggled internally for a few more months. Finally, I was in the church and the pastor said, "Has your life been exactly what you wanted it to be then one day the rug was pulled out from under you? You can't find your way, nothing is going the way you planned it? God gave you what you needed now it's time for you to do what he designed you for." I grab my clutch and I left the building. I didn't need to hear anything else. I got the message loud and clear. That started me on another shift.

The Rise

I was at a slumber party, drinking wine of course, just hanging out. I was telling stories of a loser I was dating but not happy with, yet still dating. I didn't love him and actually couldn't stand him. A young lady looked across the table at me what she said changed my life forever.

"Do you know yourself, queen?" She paused and waited for me to answer; I had none.

"Do you know you are worthy? He doesn't

deserve you! Why are you so angry?" She continued, "You are successful you are smart you are beautiful, you are funny you are amazing. Why are you so angry?" she finished in a soft voice.

The young lady looked at me, directly in my eyes. It was not a condescending look, but like an older sister. The softness in her eyes told me that it was safe to be honest. The fact was that I had not experienced this from another woman in my life.

When she said the things she did, I didn't know how to receive it. I was shocked: never had someone shown me such love... genuine love. A total stranger saw in me what I didn't see in myself.

For years I didn't think that I was smart. Yes. I graduated from design school with honors, but during my abusive relationship I was constantly told that I was
stupid, a dumb fool; He used to tell me that I would need him to survive. After hearing all this negativity poured into me for years and on a daily basis, I actually started believing it. The impact of the abuse I endured stayed with me for a decade after I left him.

The young queen from the party that night stayed up all night with me and told me about the transformational work she did. She thought I would be amazing doing the same work. She told me which classes to take and I was in the classes within two weeks--another shift towards my greatness.

The Reign

    I did the work; it was hard looking into and analyzing myself. I had to begin understanding the woman that I had become after all of the past hurt and pain that I had buried deep inside of me. I was unaware of the damage done. I was learning a new me and I must tell you after my first seminar I had breakthrough. I started doing the work to release the pain. I forgave me, the young 15-year-old Charon who didn't know any better. I forgave my abuser, forgave the people who only had negativity to pour in to me and I started pouring positivity in to myself. I praised myself that even in the mix of my pain, that love for my child pushed me to do better; I became responsible for my own happy. I started living and not just walking around in misery. I started loving me and living in my authentic truth. I got out of my own way to allow me to shine!

    I found that what made me completely happy was being a hands on Designer; I love using my hands and creating in a space of freedom. When your gift and purpose are clear to you, that's when you are able to start working toward your destiny. That is when true joy happens. I feel free for the first time in my life. Finally, I was happy, *really happy* from the depths of my soul.

    Today my blessing from God is an Attorney in 4 states. YAS HUN-TY! FOUR STATES! She is my greatest creation. I am happy, from the depths of my soul. The journey wasn't easy but it was so worth it. Embrace the stages you're in. Rise and Reign Queen! I love you to wholeness.

To embrace the true power that you hold Queen,
You must search deep within yourself,
And find the courage to go places that you have only dreamt of.
Let it be all encompassing because your journey, your transcendence is sacred.
The path you take has been carved only for your heels to trace.
Go in peace and shine your light.
It is time not to Rise & Reign.
By Audrey Malone

Dawania Brown

I call heaven and earth to record this day against you, that I have set before you, life and death, blessing and cursing: therefore choose life, that both thou and thy seed may live.

Deuteronomy 30:19

According to national statistics, one in every four women will become a victim of severe physical violence in their lifetime. That's twenty five percent of all women. These statistics are heart wrenching!

Can you imagine becoming a victim of such violence and having to FIGHT for your life while yet still INSIDE of your mother's womb? This was exactly my experience. Before I could even make my grand entrance into the world, I would be ushered into the grim world of domestic violence. While still growing inside of my mother's womb, I would endure the many challenges that come along with facing physical abuse, yet my father and I had not even been formally introduced yet. He would be the one to introduce me to a world filled with so much pain and heartbreak: a world where heated arguments regularly resulted in a bruised ego or even a bruised face; a world where deciding between throwing an object and throwing a punch was considered the norm. This was the world as I knew it; this was my reality.

Before I was ever formed in my mother's womb, God had a plan and purpose for my life. And the enemy wasn't happy about it. He must have peaked into my destiny because he wanted me dead. Let me say that one more time for the people in the back: the enemy wanted me DEAD! He knew that it would only take one person to break this vicious cycle of violence. He knew that it would only take one person to slay the very curse that had been plaguing our family for generations. He knew that it would only take one person to change our entire family tree. He knew that "the one" would be me! He knew that generations that had been riddled with pain would now be used to perfect my purpose.

The year was 1976, when cool cats and foxy mommas were sporting bell bottoms and platform shoes. When the afro was righteous and had to be patted and shaped just right. Marvin Gaye could be heard soulfully serenading the ladies with songs like "Let's Get It On" and "I Want You". Sunday afternoons were reserved for cruising around town in the family's Dodge Challenger with no specific destination in mind. The city of Philadelphia was in the midst of its Bicentennial celebration. It had been 200 years since the signing of the Declaration of Independence right there in the city of Brotherly Love. During this massive celebration, an art designer, Robert Indiana, allow the city to borrow the iconic LOVE sculpture that still sits in the city's center today. Indiana recorded that he considered "Love a one sentence poem". After all, love is a universal message, right? Universal or not, there was a young woman right there in the city who would soon learn that love simply wasn't enough.

    At the age of thirty, my mother found out that she was expecting her second child. By this time, she and my father had been married for almost a decade. They already had one son together. Although she was excited about the news, she was admittedly surprised as well. She had recently graduated from Temple University and had been focused on her new and exciting career as an elementary school teacher. She had even lost a significant amount of weight which in turn boosted her confidence and even heightened her self-esteem. She was so proud as she processed the news of having another baby; she had hoped that the news of the pregnancy would help in soothing some of the pains within the marriage. She loved my father so much and he loved her too. She thought that somehow a new baby might "fix" the relationship's issues. She thought that somehow this new baby could possibly bring a refreshing newness to the marriage. Sadly, she would soon find out that this simply wasn't the case. No matter how much she tried to make the relationship work, it seemed that it became more and more volatile. Disagreements about things that most people would consider to be insignificant would almost always result with confrontation. Combine that my father's infidelity, alcohol and drug abuse and there you have it. A whole mess! Unfortunately, it didn't matter that my mother was carrying a precious life inside of her. Together, we would be forced to fight for our lives.

At this point, I was a baby in uterus. I would have heard the ruckus and the explosive arguments. I would have even felt the force of the trauma. But I wouldn't have any conscious memory of these occurrences. By the time I was three years old, my parents were legally separated. There was no way that I would be able to recollect or recall these events in detail. So how did history repeat itself? How did I find myself repeatedly in similar physical altercations while pregnant with my first child? How was I now experiencing domestic violence as an adult? How did I find myself suffering from the same pain as my mother? How could this be happening? Certain characteristics like red hair color and the sickle cell anemia trait are passed down through your blood line. Domestic violence was passed down through mine.

My mother was a fighter. She believed in standing up for what she believed. She was also a woman who exhibited strong faith. But somehow she found herself fighting the same battle over and over. She found herself fighting the man she loved. She found herself fighting her husband. We all know a woman like that. That woman may even be you. I remember while growing up we would often joke about how my mother would pick up anything within reach to defend herself. We used to have a set of African statues sitting on the coffee table of our living room, one man and one woman. I imagined that they were husband and wife. It comes as no surprise that the woman was broken as a result of a tussle between my parents. And just like that woman, my mother was broken. Subconsciously, I became broken too. Watching my mother, I learned to become a fighter until the day that I could no longer fight. I learned to stand up for what I believed in until that day I could no longer stand. My legs became weak. It was on that day that I learned to kneel. I began submitting my heart and my life to God. I began begging for His strength to find my way. I cried out to Him for deliverance and the best part is He heard my cry. It was by His grace and His mercy that I was able to overcome.

February 4, 2010 is a day I will never forget, a day that would change my life forever. It was the beginning of the end. In Maryland, we were preparing for a historic blizzard often referred to as "Snowmageddon". This blizzard would bring with it more than three feet of snow over the course of two days. As we were preparing for this storm, another storm was brewing. My fiancé and I had what I thought to be a minor disagreement about our grocery shopping list. Seriously? Were we really arguing about buying pancake mix versus frozen waffles? It was the day before payday so we didn't have much money. We had a total of $100 that we had borrowed from a family member. This meant we had to be strategic in our attempt to be sure we had enough food for our entire household. After all, we had no way of knowing exactly how many days we would be confined to our home. However, this minor disagreement went from the store to the parking lot and somehow escalated to a scuffle on the side of the road in my SUV. This resulted in my face being scarred and hair being ripped from my scalp. I was devastated. When the police arrived, my heart sank. I never wanted him to go to jail. I just wanted him to stop hurting me. We were just four months away from what we believed was the perfect wedding date. A hefty down payment had been made to the perfect venue. I had already purchased my wedding dress and it was… you guessed it… perfect. But on this day, I was forced to face the gruesome reality that our relationship certainly was not. It was far from perfect. Like my mother, I was forced to face the fact that love simply wasn't enough. I had to acknowledge that this was a real problem that wouldn't simply vanish on its own. I had to face it head this curse head on.

    I had been hiding the abuse for months. In fact, I hid it so well that most people were utterly shocked when I began sharing the events of what happened. I became so comfortable in such an uncomfortable state. I had learned to live with the pain. I brought new meaning to the term *pain management*. I found myself saying things like "It's not all bad", "It could be worse" and "He's a great guy 99% of the time". But sadly, there was the other 1% of the time when I truly feared for my life. I went from fighting the man that I loved to fighting the (wo)man in the mirror to fighting the enemy for my crown. I began believing that somehow I deserved the abuse. Silly me. I thought somehow everything would work out and be okay. There were a handful of people who knew the abuse was taking place. I reached out to them. At the time, I couldn't understand why they weren't helping me. I was desperately crying out for help. After seeking healing for myself, I later came to the realization that I was expecting help from people who could not help me. These were people who didn't truly understand what I was going through. And in some instances, they needed healing for themselves. How could I ever expect them to give me what they didn't have?

Let's be clear. The abuse happened. It happened to my mother. It happened to many of the women in my family. It happened to me. There's absolutely nothing we can do in order to change the past. I repositioned my crown by choosing not to be ashamed to reveal the truth about what happened. Although it wasn't an easy thing to do, I had to identify the curse on my family and call it out for exactly what it was. I began recognizing that the more I shared my experiences, the more people I met who could relate. However, please know that my story isn't about the abusers. My story is about how I dug deep and gained the necessary strength to overcome this recurring obstacle. My story is about how I was able to triumph in the face of tragedy. My story is about how God turned that same pain into purpose and allows me to help inspire other women to break free too. My story is about how I had to stop the generational curse of domestic violence from passing on to my two beautiful daughters. My story is about every woman who could be subject to physical violence. My story is about YOU!

Albert Einstein is attributed with saying that

"insanity is doing the same thing over and over again and expecting different results." After years of trying, my mother finally began realizing that she couldn't continue the way she was. I had to come to the same realization years later. Although our decisions were made more than thirty years apart, we both understood that if we kept doing what we were doing that we would keep getting the results that we were getting. She recognized that she had to do what was best for her two children. I had to recognize the same for mine. I took it a step further. I had to do even more than what my mother had been willing to do. I had to seek more than just an escape from the situation.

    I never wanted to experience this hurt again. I had to ensure that my daughters would never experience this pain. I sought out deliverance, not just for me, but for my entire bloodline. I desired healing from the inside out. In my search, I found the unconditional love of God. Experiencing His love showed me how to begin loving myself. Through extensive counseling, I was able to identify the source of the pain and work to bind up the wounds. The wounds were deeply rooted in years of abuse, neglect and mistrust. I found that I had misplaced anger as well. I was angry with my father for the repeated abuse of my mother and the neglect of us as his children. In order to heal, I had to make a conscious effort to forgive him. I mean *really* forgive him. I began recognizing that all of the men I had ever dated or married were just another version of my father. Forgiveness wasn't for him though; forgiveness was for me! I submitted the broken pieces of me to the Lord. His love mended me and made me whole.

No matter what you may be experiencing today, know that God can and will do the same for you. No matter what has caused your crown to shift, He loves you so much. There's nothing you can ever do to stop that. He helped me to reposition my crown so I know He'll do the same for you. Submit the broken pieces of your life to Him. Ask Him for guidance. Experience His unconditional love. Thank Him for His new mercies. Bask in His amazing grace. Know that it's okay to ask for help. Speak with a counselor. Do your best. Take it one day at a time. Most importantly, know that you are absolutely beautiful, both inside and out. And it is never okay for anyone to hurt you, EVER!

Your crown may shift, but never let it fall. Reposition your crown, Queen, because you truly deserve it all! Now it's time to tell the enemy to RUN ME MY CROWN!

Eleshia Best Thomas

Through my truth and transparency my legacy as well as myself will be healed, delivered and set free from all generational curses.

John 8:32

Eleshia Rosina Best was born full of confidence, passion, affection and boldness She had dreams of becoming a traveling actress so that she could share her gifts with the world. Yes, that was me. I grew up living with two working parents and two siblings in a rather nice row house in west Baltimore city. I even had all four of my grandparents growing up, along with the most supportive aunt and uncle. They actually lived in close proximity right around the corner from my home.

This sounds like such a blessing, right? Unfortunately, this was not the case. How did I, this *privileged* young girl, grow up feeling lost, unappreciated and unloved. I had such a desire to be noticed and to receive affection--especially from my mother. Yet, I received criticism, negativity, doubt and fear. My mother would not hold me and she didn't tell me that she loved me. When I gained weight, she always reminded me and made me feel awful instead of helping me to lose weight. She always found something wrong with my clothes or my appearance. I was the girl who was drowning in the pressure of not disappointing my family that I did not even feel that I belonged to. I strived so hard to please everyone but I still never felt that I was good enough or even capable of accomplishing anything.

I often started things and didn't finish them due to a lack of support or encouragement. As a result, I started dance and high school band but quit both by my senior year. I even started college in 1996 and didn't finish until 2011. Support was needed.

Always feeling rejection and distance put me in a state of loneliness and depression. As a result I began a journey to seek attention, love and self-worth. It felt and looked as if no one was even watching or cared. How could I have all of this family around me and not one person notice all of the pain I was feeling? How could they not see my fear of not ever finding love or the hurt of not being accepted? Day after day my actions were screaming for attention. *Look at me, Look at me!!*

I was a good girl, no behavior problems, belonged to a church, attended school and I had plenty of friends. The one thing that I was lacking, the one thing that I did not have yet so desired, was a true transparent honest mother and daughter relationship with my mom. Even though my mother and I resided in the same household we were spiritually strangers. *What is it, mommy?* I wondered to myself. Why doesn't she ask me how my day was? Why doesn't she kiss or hug me when I am leaving for school or when sending me to bed? Why doesn't she tell me that she is proud of me or that she loves me? Why doesn't she tell me how to be a respectable woman, what to avoid when it comes to men, how to be a lady and what it truly means to be a Queen? *Why mommy? What is it?* I just could not figure out what had been stopping her from loving me, her daughter.

Unfortunately my mother never answered this unasked question, but Jesus did. Jesus gently whispered to me one day when Eleshia, the woman, showed up and was ready to handle the answer and was hungry for change. Jesus said to me, "It is the secrets, Eleshia." *Secrets? What secrets, Lord?* The ones that women carry hidden so far beneath the surface that they do not even realize that they are even there; the things that only you and I know about and never discuss. *Wow. Ok, Lord I'm ready. I am ready for you to show me, me.*

A mothers secrets are a curse to her seed. It brings harm and hurt to her legacy and a huge hindrance to her family and personal growth. While using all of her energy to suppress a deep, dark, painful secret or secrets, she learns how to cope with this pain through lies, manipulation, fake emotions and fantasies. Consistently tucking away her reality in the recess of her mind instead of allowing the truth to set her free. The generational habit of keeping secrets can become a part of a family's bloodline; it becomes a part of the DNA. The only way to remove the curse and put a permanent end to a repetitive, poisonous curse is to first face and acknowledge the root of the sickening. Where did this poison come from? Where did it originate?

It first started in my past. I was taught to keep secrets as a child. I was exposed to things that as a child I should not have experienced. I was told that "whatever happens in this house stays in this house". This type of behavior led me to believe that it was ok to keep secrets. It showed me and made me believe that it was also ok to tell a lie. This not only became my norm but it now was a contagious cycle. I was now able to take a look at my past and I began to see a pattern of secrets that caused me to make one unwise choice after another.

Making the choice to hook school in the seventh grade with a friend turned into me having a traumatic experience. I thought I was just skipping school; never in a million years would I have thought I would return home that day to become victim of rape. Holding on to the secret of being raped caused me to fall prey to a promiscuous lifestyle. Most people would think that after experiencing rape that I would have hated sex. Nope. I used sex to receive the attention that I was lacking and to manipulate men into giving me the material things that I couldn't afford and wasn't able to get at home.

Two years after this incident a close adult friend of my family attempted to rape me while my best friend was sleeping in the same room with me. Thankfully this time I was able to fight my rapist off and they begged me to keep this a secret and said that they would get therapy. All I could do is think to myself was *why me?* A person that I trusted, that I considered to be family would go as far as to pull down my underwear and penetrate me. How could they violate me in such a way and then ask me not to tell? I was devastated. I was so familiar with keeping secrets that I became comfortable and just tucked this secret away as well. Gone, like it never even happened.

I attempted to block out all of my trauma and transferred the hurt into more dysfunction. I began to idolize money to the point of no return. I chased and I chased and I chased, hoping to one day fill a void that only Jesus Christ could fill; at the time, I had no idea. Years went by and I continued to make mistake after mistake, bad choice after bad choice. I did not know that Jesus was right there beside me as I continued to ruin my life. He was waiting for me to hand my life over but I was not ready. I was comfortable in my mess, yet Jesus continue to cover me and wait on me to get tired of my trifling behavior. I felt the love of God through every wrong that I faced but instead of submitting I ran. Ran from man to man, situation to situation.

I once thought to myself *I have finally arrived.* I thought I had found a man that could fulfill all of my material and sexual needs on a whole new level. This had to be it. I thought everything would be good from that point forward. This fantasy quickly crumbled as soon as he became abusive to me physically and mentally. I couldn't believe that the man I made my husband and gave his first and only son, could talk down to me--treat me like trash. *Why Lord? How much more can I take?* I did know that the Lord was with me. I could feel his presence and I knew that I could call on His name and that He would answer and help me out of my mess.

Once I truly acknowledged God and who he was and the fact that I needed him, the healing began. Acknowledging and facing the truth to my past allowed me to start a healing process that included reaching and calling out to Jesus, letting him know that I was ready to face my past. I wanted to know the truth about what caused me to want to live such a dark life and not the life that He had created me for me to live. I was finally tired of keeping secrets. I realized that keeping secrets was the root to all of my pain, misery, doubt and fear.

I began to pray daily in addition to attending a great bible based church; it was such a great feeling to meditate on the Word of God. I learned how to seek the face of God and dwell in His presence for all of the answers to the questions I kept asking. I was able to surrender to the will of God wholeheartedly. I began to be hopeful and saw purpose for my life. I was now able to walk in God's will for my life, which caused me to find my purpose so that I could live on purpose. I learned how to activate and stand on the word of God and protect my faith. I now knew how to make better choices for my life and my children through walking with Christ. I finally knew my worth:

I am a daughter of a King.
I am royalty.
I am the head and not the tail.
I am above and not beneath.
I am who God says I am.
I am worthy.

    I began to love me because I understood that Christ loved me so much that He laid down his life for me. Through the free gift of salvation, I learned that I didn't have to give up my body to anyone. My body is a temple and I had to honor God through how I treated my body. I was able to identify why my mother and I didn't have a loving relationship--she could only give me what she had. I understood that my mom gave me the best that she could give. She provided for me and gave me the domestic skills that I have today. I am very grateful for the relationship that my mother and I now have. There is always space for growth, but my mom is now aware of how I feel and how she and I can do better. I am now able to forgive the rapists and anyone else who violated or did me wrong in the past. I decided that I wanted to live! The days of keeping secrets end with me. I can confide in and trust Jesus with all of my burdens, all of my secrets. I have finally found a safe place where I am not ashamed of my imperfections. I feel accepted, loved and appreciated. The love of God is beyond trustworthy, always available and faithful. I have finally found the peace, joy and comfort that I had been searching for in all of the wrong places. I did not find it in the world and I understand that the world cannot take it away.
    I was able to take back every single thing and

more that I allowed the enemy to steal through secrets. My life and my legacy were depending on me to break free from living in silence. I am the answered prayer of my ancestors. I will live in my truth.

Remember that you are able to take back your crown, your power, by living in your truth. The enemy has no power once you break free from being captive and bound to secrets. He cannot hold anything over your life once you face it, heal from it, and tell it. There is beauty in brokenness. Through truth and transparency you can become FREE!

Joi Hayward

So do not throw away your confidence; it will be richly rewarded..

Hebrews 10:35

It was the summer of 2002 and I was a third wheel for a potential date. My girlfriend had been working with a young man for a few weeks and they were meeting at a pool hall. She invited me to attend in hopes I would meet someone new. She described her friend as handsome and intelligent. She said he was the kind of guy that was very smart but tried to play himself down to fit in with the cool crowd.

When we entered the pool hall, I found out the guy she was meeting with actually worked at this pool hall! My first thought was that he was a hustler. He finished college, worked a day job, and had a night job too. He was also easy on the eyes. My second thought was he must have a friend. I was not really looking for anything because "I needed to be found", but I thought to myself this night has potential.

At that time I had just become committed to attending church and cultivating a relationship with the Lord. I heard I should not be looking for a husband because as the scripture says, "He who finds a wife..." So, I had to hide and be found.

It was an interesting night indeed. After meeting this young man I was introduced to his brother. However, the brother and I were a complete strikeout. As a matter of fact, the thought of dating the brother put me in the mindset of a Biggie Smalls anthem - "Get Money" - because all he talked about was what he could buy me.

The evening was quite painful while the brother was still there. But as soon as he left I started to have a great time even as the third wheel. I played pool with my girlfriend's friend. I played before, but this guy was serious competition. I had lots of fun playing while my girlfriend sat to the side being her usual cute self. I actually won the first game but I lost every game after that. I often wonder if he let me win the first game to make the night fun.

When the night was over, I thought to myself, "*I have to come back.*" I am going to learn to be the best female pool player. I am going to work on my game then come back and beat this guy. Maybe I will even join the team.

Two weeks later I went to the pool hall alone. I had to brace myself because the brother (Mr. Big Bucks) was a part owner of the establishment. I felt I might have to interact with him, but I was determined to just get in there and hone my skills. On the way there, I went to the local corner store and picked up my usual drink, Sky Blue. I put my drink in a brown paper bag and grabbed a few cups. The night had potential.

At this point of my life it seemed my cute, young self was having trouble meeting guys who were about anything more than money, drugs and hooking up. I played the part of the trophy girlfriend, the drug dealer's girlfriend, and the thug's girlfriend. And no matter how many gifts given, trips I went on, or fancy restaurants I was wined and dined in, I knew I didn't want to play those games any more.

Pause here. There is another story inside of my story… A year before this happened I met a guy at church who I thought was very nice. I thought we could have had a good thing until I had a very strange experience hanging out at his house.

I drove about an hour to get there. It was a Friday night and I had been working all day. I had a splitting headache so I asked him if I could have some Advil or Tylenol. He gave me Tylenol. However, soon after I took it I fell fast asleep. I woke up the next morning fully dressed, but to this day, I do not remember anything else from that evening. Strange right. That was the last time I hung out with that guy. I share this to say I was striking out with meeting guys everywhere even at church.

Ok, back to the pool hall... I have my drink in a brown paper bag with two cups as I was prepared to share. I went into the pool hall and the brother was not there. YES!!! But guess who was? My girlfriend's friend, my new nemesis. He gave me my table for free. Then he told me to give him a few minutes because he was coming down from the booth to play with me.

As he got ready to come to play with me, I noticed he had been reading a book. He sat it aside and came down and schooled me repeatedly. Then he became my teacher. He showed me how to play the game strategically. Then he showed me the trophies he had won in a recent tournament. Can you believe it? I was playing a professional.

We played all night. I sat down at the table to relax and have a few sips from my brown paper bag. He sat down at the table with me and as we began to talk, I observed that he wasn't only a college graduate, but highly intelligent.

I asked him about what he had been reading and he brought his books over. He showed me what he'd been reading when I came in, a book called the Buffalo Soldier. Then he told me that this book, Buffalo Soldier, had nothing on the great book as he showed me The Holy Bible. I threw my brown paper bag into the garbage to give this young man my undivided attention. He talked to me until 3 o'clock in the morning.

When I was leaving he asked me if I could call him when I got home so he would know I got home safely. I accepted his phone number and called him when I got home.

After that night, we became good friends. It

was easy to hang out with him. It was relaxing to talk to him. I even visited his family's church.

Weeks later I had to tell my girlfriend that we started "talking" and it led to dating. It was an awful and awkward situation. I felt like the terrible friend who started dating her friend's boyfriend behind her back. This situation certainly caused some distance between us. It also put distance between me and other friends.

I'll skip a few pages in the story and tell you 9 months after I met this guy I married him.

Start Right and Finish Right or Start Wrong and Finish Right

I can't exactly say I am proud of how this all got started. I can also tell you the story got worse before it got better. Not many believed we would amount to much. I soon found out my new husband did not think we could amount to much either.

Two months after we married, I was pregnant with our first child. One month later we moved to Germany. One month after the move he wanted to send me back to my parents. He felt like he didn't know what he got himself into and at that point nor did I.

The night before I flew back to my parents we sat on the bed and cried about the fact that I was returning home, My husband, at 24 was headed to Iraq for a year, I would experience the pregnancy without him and a year from that day we would decide if this marriage was the right thing to do. At 23 and 24 this was craziness to deal with.

When he returned home from Iraq the

following year. He was different, he was more on fire for the Lord and was surely in love with his 5-month-old daughter he had just met. But he was not in love with me. He barely looked at me when he spoke to me. He spent countless hours at work. I felt like he didn't want to be in the home with me. Dartanion, my husband, was extremely distant and showed no need for me to be around except to be a mother to his child.

He accepted me but I am sure he was just trying to do the right thing.
Our daily life constantly reminded me of words people said to me and about me like, *"How could a relationship last that started the way it did?"* and *"If he cheated to be with you, he will also cheat on you."*

In my mind, this was the typical story of the other woman. Condemnation sat beside me every day. I was convinced my husband desired a different life to include a different wife. I anticipated him having another life somewhere. After months of paranoia, I was ready to pack up and leave. I was willing to deal with every lecture and all the chants of "I told you so."

On the day of my planned departure, I went to the bank to clean out the banking account. I needed funds to be able to stay on my feet while I went through the transition. I also wanted to hurt him and it seemed like spending "his" money was the only way I could do so since I did not work. I wrote myself a major check and I packed up my daughter and was about to make an exit.

On my way to pick up my daughter, I ran into the pastor of our church. He cordially asked me how I was doing. As I tried to cover up everything that was going on, I believe the Lord Himself came to visit me through my pastor. I never told my pastor my intentions but he ministered to me in a way that gave me my fight back. The words he spoke to me gave me hope and caused me to dig my heels in the ground and go to war for my family.

I loved my husband and I loved having my family growing together in the same location. My husband was acting up. He was throwing me away daily, but all I needed was a word from God to know this fight was already won.

First, I had some apologizing to do. I had to call my friend and let her know I was sorry for what I did; for how things transpired between us. I had to come clean within myself; no longer justifying that how my husband and I started dating was the right way to start any kind of married life. I had to locate myself and begin to defy everything that came against me to discourage me and plant seeds of insecurity. I had to woman-up, wife-up and mom-up. Despite the hurt I was enduring, and the unfairness I experienced, I had to move forward. I had to keep it together and stop throwing ugly words and bringing up conversations about the past. I had to get through my pregnancy with the least amount of self-inflicting and external stress to have a healthy baby and take the best care of my almost two-year old daughter. I had to commit myself to focusing on the goodness of the Lord until I could see the goodness He had for me in this life.

My turnaround did not happen overnight. But one night after my husband experienced The Real Men's Conference in Heidelberg, Germany, he came back- different. He returned home with a new zeal for

God, his children and his wife. He apologized for all the times he hurt me and declared he would never do it again. He committed himself to loving me as Christ loved the church.

I am now on a mission to help others believe God first. If I had listened to those around me or if I had listened to Dartanion himself, I could have thrown away the life I now live. I am so glad someone gave me the Word of God and God's heart towards my marriage during the times of adversity. It gave me sustaining hope. My hope then caused me to lean more of God's abilities. Finally, I was able to stand on the Word I heard and began to understand. This same Word bottled my tears, healed my scars, and set me on a path of ever-increasing love in my marriage.

I can stand before any person today, and confidently declare I am happily, affectionately, and purposefully married. My marriage is divorce proof. We celebrated fourteen years of marriage as of 2017. We now have a worldwide ministry helping other families, individuals and marriages.

"Your confidence in God will attract the manifestation of everything He has already granted you."
- Joi Hayward

Keona Jones

Through my truth and transparency my legacy as well as myself will be healed, delivered and set free from all generational curses.

John 8:32

Come close. May I tell you secret, more like a series of secrets? This will be the story of how I took myself from childhood failure to a striving for success. I'm going to share with you something that I have very seldom shared with anyone out loud. This explains my motive, my reason for living, and what propels me. This will be a swan dive into love, loss, regret, and redemption. Take a journey into self-actualization with me.

"How could you? I'm so disappointed. You should've known better. What are people going to think? This is so embarrassing! You're never going to live this down". All of these were thoughts swirling around my head as I sat on the steps brokenhearted with tears streaming down my face. I was in the 11th grade and things felt just about perfect until about three months ago. I was called to the office to explain why the blood wouldn't stop flowing. Somebody had to have an explanation of why I have been going through the health issues that I was dealing with.

Devastation, disappointment, and most of all I felt that I was a disgrace. I felt like I had disgraced my mother, who had been working my whole life to take care of me by herself. She would never understand how I let something so foolish happened to myself. Even worse than that I had no words to explain it.

Prior to getting the phone call I knew. I've been extremely in tune with my body, every time something changed I noticed, whether I said so or not. I had conversations with one of my closest friends about what would happen if I would be pregnant or what would happen if they were pregnant, how do they think their parents would react? I thought it was all hypothetical I had no idea that I was foreshadowing what was coming in my next few weeks.

Being 16 years old I didn't know enough about the world to be able to make this type of adult decision. This decision was too heavy, and anymore wrong decisions would haunt me my whole life. God made the decision for me. I wasn't ready at all to be a mother but I knew I didn't have the strength to go on with an abortion or adoption. I was in a state of confusion, not knowing what to do but thankful that things are moving on whether I chose a standstill or not.

Where do you hide when you've made a bad decision and the consequences are fatal? I couldn't really discuss it with too many people. My embarrassment was mounting. I knew people would say it was my own fault, and couldn't forgive myself. I thought my mother would never forgive me either. I tucked the guilt deep down in my heart and it stayed hidden until he couldn't stay buried for any longer.

Loneliness made me make horrible decisions, he had jet black curly hair with dark skin and now in my memory the rest of his face is shadows. I wasn't really interested in him; it was just something to pass the time. Suggesting that we hook up with only sort of a joke, how could I have known that would've come from it. I don't think he would actually show up anyway. He was from the other side of the tracks and I was sort of intrigued by that. I felt nothing more than curiosity. Seems curiosity killed the cat and a lot of my innocence that day as well.

I knew it was a bad idea I didn't know him well but I knew that I shouldn't of been involved with him in the first place. I finally gained my whit, called him to cancel, and told him not to come because I had changed my mind. But by then he said it was too late he claimed he was around the corner and was just going to stop by and say hello. Always follow your always follow your intuition.

We met at the meeting place and we were together for no more than 15 minutes total. Can you believe in 15 minutes a whole person's life to be changed, and in that 15 minutes I was on the phone with a girlfriend trying to give him the appearance that I was not interested at all. It turns out that that didn't matter he came to be grown and I just wasn't ready. I told Him that I didn't want to, I asked him to stop but he just kept going. He ignored my request, ignored my demands. In my mind I thought to fight him but he was so much bigger than I was then I would've been brutally raped instead of just being taken advantage of. At that time, I didn't see it as me being raped, I thought as a consequence for a bad decision. I attempted to push him off of me he was double my size and definitely overpowered me the only thing that interrupted his trust thing was when his thoughts. He said to me "I better stop because I don't want to get you pregnant." The irony of it all, I guess somehow he knew what he was doing. I was 16 and didn't quite understand all the mechanics of it all. I didn't think about the fact that it only takes one second of a slip to make a mistake to last a lifetime. After he was satisfied and got what he wanted he got up, casually said he would call me later and before he could finish the sentence I closed the door.

Filled with anger self-loathing and disappointment, I tucked the way the pain and I try to act like it never happened. My cycle is pretty normal so when he continued on interrupted I thought I was clear. No issues I can just act like this never happened and forget it. I was wrong. Three months after my bad decision a life was lost. I was ill-equipped to handle such an adult decision. My mother was devastated and my head was in a cloud of confusion.

Remembering all that I have been through over

the last four months, I sat on the marble steps and just cried. My mother came to pick me up from school it seemed like the car ride to the doctor's office took an eternity. She was crying, I was crying, I felt like this was the worst thing that ever could've happened to me. Each of my tears was an apology, my face was covered in apology and regret. Her tears were declarations of fear for me, the situation I have gotten myself into, and worry about how we were going to get out. She didn't abandon me but I felt like she should've. I suppose I would've understood if she turned her back on me I made a horrible decision and it was mine that I should've dealt with alone. It was at this point that I noticed the quiet strength of a mother. She was disappointed and of course didn't agree with my actions but she stood by my side and supported me anyway

I told myself to move on never think about the events that happened again but somehow that's the lingered in my heart and in my soul. I was on my senior retreat and we were told to do some sort of assignment by the letter to somebody that you really cared about I chose you. Choose to write a letter to you apologizing how I had not been mature enough to receive you and vowed that I would be successful going forward in life if only just because you were watching. I need you Alexis well I knew that I couldn't take care of you and wasn't really ready to be a mother I still named you affectionately anyway.

Forgiveness comes in many forms. I hadn't forgiven or forgotten my past but I thought going away to college was a fresh start. I felt like I have been waiting for college my whole life. The energy of newness, new surroundings, new environment, and new people all of which excited me. I was nervous I was looking forward to the opportunity to start my life over again. No one knew my past, nobody knew my secrets, and there were no preconceived notions of who I was. I could reinvent myself. I could be exactly what I wanted to be, not known as the out-of-control party girl not seen is the girl who had a past, but I could be the career driven intellectual that I needed to be as an adult I definitely enjoy most of my childhood it was time to mature and prepare for my future. Before I could get all the way on the campus I met "him". The "him" that my mother told me do not come back from college with. The exact man of my mother told me I should keep my focus from and keep my entire focus on my professional and academic life. He was new and exciting and his energy matched mine, at that exact moment I thought he was my soul mate. My encounters with him represented Philadelphia to me as a whole. Everything I knew of the cit, everything I loved, and embraced was part of our experience. I relationship was filled with art, music, culture, and passion everything that felt alive and vibrant. As love stories, go this one came to an end, but not before I conceived my second child. Considering the ordeal of being forced into conception, when I got pregnant this time I decided I would be responsible, rearrange my life, and except the blessing as it came. Not many in my life supported my decision, the closest people to me believed that having a child at this stage of my life will have a negative impact. They couldn't conceptualize my strength or my determination to be successful by any means necessary. So I strapped my baby to my back continued and fought my way through my last few courses. I graduated regardless of what the naysayers believed with my daughter there to witness.

Love didn't provide the happily ever after, please forgive me for trying again. He was what I thought dreams are made of. I supported him in his dreams, I thought he understood that I had a mission and a purpose as well. He was a member of a prominent family, a member of a prestigious fraternity and seemed to be a walking embodiment of a perfect husband. We enjoyed our time together, he was younger and had a bit of a sense of adventure that I appreciated. He had a hidden youthful wild streak that connected me desires I never knew I had. He provided a quiet fire that I was determined to feel the heat of for the rest of my life. We got married and I later discovered that he was not ready to be exclusive. I thought this was my forever husband and my heart had been broken. I had left my family my career and everything that I've valued to start a life with him in another state. Away from my family and every piece of my support system, emotionally and financially I had to depend on him. An invaluable lesson was learned through that dependency. It seemed like things were going well but the responsibility of being a husband and a father was too much for him. He enjoyed the freedom of being single and so while I was building a home and a life for us, he was sleeping with people that called themselves "our" friends.

I went to go drop off Kayla to her father for the summer came back to find my husband was no longer my husband. I was excited to spend some time with him one on one but the drive home from the airport was awkward. He told me he wanted a divorce and this wasn't the first time. but I didn't Believe him I just thought we were having a difficult time and that marriage counseling would help. After an outward hour long ride home from Atlanta we finally got to the house and I began unpacking. I walked up to him and he look me in my eyes with a cold look that I had never seen on his face before. He looked through me and said, "I don't love you anymore."

I remembered him and us. I laid there in a bit of an abyss, wallowing in my own sorrow, unsure of how my forever life have been so short and so temporary. Back in the bed that was my childhood bad in the home that I grew up and I was putting the pieces of my life back together. My life was on auto pilot for a while because emotionally I was completely bankrupt. Somehow God just carried me because I'm absolutely sure I wasn't putting one foot in front of the other. This was one of the instances where I was being pulled through life as opposed to forging through it on my own. Laying there with tears in my eyes and a massive weight on my heart, I felt like I was dying. My daughter laid beside me, banging on my chest, giving me figurative CPR. She was resuscitating me, reminding me that as long as I had air in my lungs and blood running through my veins that I had a mission. She broke my trance, I gathered the shattered prices of my heart, soul, and life and began the process of moving on.

She is my mission, my purpose and my drive. Every day I think of ways and situations to be authentically inspiring to her. I want her to be proud, compassionate, confident, intelligent, and driven to greatness. People either want to be carbon copies of their parents or the polar opposite. I find her emulating me in her daily life. It's so endearing, to know that the person that I live my life for respects me enough to want to look, relate, and move like me. When she was 5, she seemed to love the idea of Barbie's look and life, very main stream and superficial. While beauty comes in all forms, authenticity is most important to me. I wanted that trait to be passed on to my daughter. I made the decision to transition to my natural hair for her. I thought if she saw me enjoy natural hair, that she would find beauty in herself. Living my life as an example for hers forced me to be a better person. Everything in me wanted to be selfish, live only for myself.

    I've always loved the notion of freedom, free to roam, explore, concur, or tear up the world. Laughably or laudably that was what used to fuel me. I've been responsible my whole life and for much of it I have been responsible for my academics, my parental responsibilities, and my financial obligations. Now that my daughter is a teen, I have had a rebirth of sorts. My thoughts were wrong all these years. I believed that having a child would tie me down, but she propelled me to new heights and new levels of awareness. Passports in hand I plan to show her the world. My mother gave me the world; my goal is for my daughter to experience all the culture the world has to offer. My daughter gave me direction; I plan to give her a global competitive edge. Our relationship has its share of ups and downs but she is one of my best friends and she embodies the best parts of me. As I strive to be my best self, because she's always watching, forgiveness came in increments. Forging my way through my life and leading hers, I found forgiveness along the path. Have you forgiven yourself?

LaKita Stewart-Thompson

Loving myself has been the hardest thing I've ever had to do.

Anonymous

Have you ever survived something? To survive means to live in spite of challenging circumstances that should have destroyed you. I believe that if you have breath in your body and are able to read this at this moment, you have survived something in this life.

My name is Lakita Stewart-Thompson and I am a survivor. A survivor of low self-worth, abandonment, abuse on many levels, rejection, self-mutilation, suicidal attempts/thoughts, depression, alcohol, and much more. Being able to survive many things has pushed me into my passion and purpose. I desire to empower and encourage anyone going through life altering situations and circumstances by sharing my story and inspiring others to do the same. I am extremely blessed for this opportunity to share a part of my journey on how life tried to steal my self-worth. I did not know who I was for a very long time. As a matter of fact, I despised and hated myself. I was my biggest critic and own enemy. I minimized myself on several levels to gain approval of others. But I thank God that he spared my life. I count it a privilege and an honor to be able to share with you as a survivor, alongside some other very powerful Queens in this book.

Suicide Attempt

I came home from school and ran straight to the medicine cabinet. There, I found bottles of prescription and over-the-counter medicines. At the age of 13, I decided, I no longer had a reason to live. I wanted to go to a place of peace and never return. I opened every bottle in the medicine cabinet and poured pills from each bottle until my hands were full. I grabbed a glass of Sunkist Orange soda and shoved two handfuls of pills down my throat. I jumped in bed and anticipated never opening my eyes again. I woke up faint and barely able to lift my head. I am not sure how I ended up in the hospital but I was just sitting there waiting my turn. Then all of sudden, I began to vomit uncontrollably what seemed like everything I ate for the entire month. As if it couldn't get any worse, a family member whispered in my ear, "you didn't try hard enough". In this moment, I felt worthless and like a complete failure; however, what should have transpired did not.

I survived.

Although my plan to die was altered by what I grew to understand as grace and mercy; that day, that particular time, after hearing those heart-breaking words, a part of my inner soul died and remained dead for many, many years thereafter. I was a broken little girl who became a wounded dysfunctional woman who was alive but not living. I was simply just existing. I felt like shattered glass.

Shattered Glass

Remembering the darkness that rested in my soul
Where brightness did not illuminate
And lightness could not communicate
Mesmerized and sedated by the physiological realm of some inner realities
Simply existing but clearly resisting
The fact that I was just lost
Depressed

A glass
In a cupboard
Once shattered into pieces
But simply glued back together again
With facades, broken promises,
Misunderstandings and lies
Broken on every side was I
Never the same
Rejected and Abandoned
Just simply placed in a box where filthy hands often came
But in that cupboard I remained
All cracked up but still being used
Most of the time I sat empty and sometimes this glass was half full
Could never be filled I was informingly confused
Visibly exposed but quietly in pain
Internally drenched with ice cubes of shame
Overwhelmingly divulged with blame though washed and bleached in what felt like flames
Flames that overcame my mind
Contaminated
Remember I am a glass
Completely Broken
So fragile was I
Not made in China
But I wore that disguise
Being filled with contents that my creator denies
Sitting in the cupboard all I could do is cry
As long as I sat there I believed every last lie
That I was shattered to pieces, broken, and not able to be fixed
So I lost my identity in the mix
Abused

Every crack and every crevice exposed me
Damaged me emotionally
I wonder if the other broken glasses in the cupboard would speak
I want to know that when they are filled do they too leak
Do they too feel weak and seek to been thrown to the floor
Did they feel less useful and not to be drank from anymore
Suicidal and worthless
As I sat in the cupboard
I remember being picked up by unknown hands
I remember never wanting to be used again
I was simply just a glass in a cupboard
But I had to identify my self-worth
So I when began reflecting on my shattered pieces
I discovered that yes I have cracks and I have crevices
And yes I may leak at times
But I am a vessel that can be used despite my abnormalities
I was once shattered but now I'm alive
I survived.

Low Self-Worth

    My journey to self-esteem, self-worth, and self-discovery took me on a tumultuous path of feeling unloved and searching for it in all the wrong places, to finding love and forgiveness through my Father so that I could break the generational curse upon my family and generations to come. I have come to realize that my journey was marked for greatness. We all experience some kind of pain, trial, or tribulation before we discover who we really are and the power we possess.

Every woman, young or old, wants to feel loved, especially from the very ones (family and loved ones) that are supposed to love you. I found myself searching for love in several unhealthy relationships. I remember putting myself in dangerous situations just for the attention. To include: being promiscuous, fighting, running away from home, drinking, and being extremely rebellious. I remember slitting my wrist hoping I would bleed to death. I left home for days at a time, sometime catching buses or taxis anywhere I could to just get away. As young as 7 years of age, I remember getting into cars with strangers. I got in many stranger's beds for love. I contemplated several times driving over a bridge. Only the Lord knows, why I am still here. In this day in time, no telling where I would be.
I survived.

Love

My perception of love was distorted at a very young age. Love meant being touched inappropriately and forced into sexual deeds. For many years' nightmares haunted me and I was afraid to sleep. I would wake up with scars from fighting myself. In my mind rejection and abandonment was normal. I saw no purpose in being loyal or staying in relationships because I lacked the capacity to trust. It was easy for me to walk away from anything and anyone. I expected to be abandoned, disrespected, and rejected. The first man that claimed he loved me, I married and my life plummeted in a direction I didn't think I could

recover from. However, there is a test in every testimony and purpose for all pain. My reality of suffering in silence kept me in bondage for years; not understanding that broken girls, ultimately become wounded women.
But, I survived

Depression

Depression and low self-worth tried to define me majority of my life. Drinking alcohol became a Band-Aid for all my problems. It helped me get through anxiety and many fears. It wasn't until after 30 years of age that I realized I was living in a state of depression. Age 13 stuck out so significantly to me because I felt so undervalued and unworthy of living. What I didn't understand back then is that the unresolved issues leading up to the age 13 is the reason I felt so low. I was suffering in silence and it was eating me up inside and out which led me down a road of hell. I experienced bouts of depression and many nightmares. Sometimes I felt okay and other times I felt like taking myself out off and on for years. In those dark moments, I did everything I could to hurt myself.

I was on a path of self-destruction and open doors that I had no idea would nearly destroy me. I felt shattered on every side. Razor blades, alcohol, drugs, sex, overdosing and suicide attempts were ways I thought I could just override the pain deep within my soul. I had become a person I never imagined becoming. Life will train you to either live or die; love or hate; succeed or fail.

I didn't wake up at 13 years of age and decide

that not living was more important than living, it stemmed from several issues gone unresolved and suffering in silence. It was a result of not speaking up when I was sexually violated, watching a family member do drugs and offer me a crack pipe, verbal, mental and physical abuse, and much more.

I survived.

Destiny

It took a failed marriage for me to deal with some suppressed realities about myself and my haunting past. Though I've experienced greater pain, this particular failure hurt me the most. It uncovered every one of my insecurities. It triggered some very deep pain that I buried unconsciously. It triggered some very deep pain that I buried unconsciously. I couldn't even have intimate moments with my "husband" because any familiar actions of my past would trigger memories that would bring disgust to my mind. Imagine enjoying an intimate moment with your spouse but a vivid image of a time you were violated runs across your mind. I would have images so vivid that I would completely shut down and begin to weep during intercourse. This brought about frustration in the bedroom and friction within the home. This ended in a divorce. However, I was impregnated with purpose. She was a blessing in disguise. My destiny, Destinee. She gave me a reason to live. She was the closest thing to God's love.

The way my life was headed, God had a plan that altered mine. I never understood unconditional love until she entered my world. I believe that God knows what we need and who we need. He makes no mistakes and orders every last one of our steps. It never makes sense while we are going through it. My past tried to remind me of how worthless I was. As a result, motherhood didn't come so easy for me. However, her smile changed my frown. The opportunity to care for this little soul was only by God's divine appointment. This little beautiful soul was sent to tear down the walls of generational curses. So the enemy wanted to destroy us both.

But I survived, so destiny (Destinee) could live.

Self-Realization

As I reflect on the many things that stole my identity, they all took a toll on how I viewed myself. I spent many, many years trying to find the lost girl within. It wasn't until I was introduced to a man named Jesus Christ that I began to realize who I really was. Learning who I really was gave me the wisdom love me for me. Understanding God's love change my entire life and changed how I viewed myself. My grandmother was a very spiritual women and church was a part of my family's weekly routine but I didn't know God for myself. I knew of Him but not enough to have a relationship.

When my relationship with Christ grew I learned a few benefits of letting go of pain:

1. It releases YOU from people and things that may have hurt you
2. It releases PEOPLE. There is truly power in forgiveness. Once we ask God for forgiveness, we can forgive others and

ourselves. Don't allow hurt to keep you in bondage. Something I use to hear often in life, "Hurt people, hurt people."
3. It releases your purpose and gives you the freedom to walk in your passion. With embracing the very things that tried to destroy me, I began to understand that all things work together for my good. Everything thing that transpired in my life was necessary.

As a result of allowing God to work in me, I realized my purpose. No matter what you've gone through or even going through, God is able. No matter how much you think you are not important God loves you! There is hope! You have a purpose! The very test you endure will determine that purpose. So whatever area in life you are being challenged in, understand that He is preparing you for your next steps in life. Your pain was specifically designed to bring out the purpose in you. My purpose has become my passion.

My message to all those who are reading is that you are only defined by what you allow to define you. Your self-esteem, self-worth, and self-discovery are in knowing that you were created by God and He loves you more than anything. He created you before the foundation of the world and knew how to mold you and make you for His glory. He knew you before you were implanted in your mother's womb. You are fearfully and wonderfully made. His love is unfailing. Everything you endure is not for you but to help someone else. You are worth it. Your of your greatest hurts will come from those you love. On the other hand, your greatest success is a result of the very things that caused the most hurt and pain. Your experiences make you who you are and will drive you into your purpose. God will never give you something to great for you to handle. Never deflate who you are to gain from others what only God can give you.

As the Repositioned Queen of Self-Worth, I am a woman who is clothed with strength and dignity; can laugh at the days to come because I understand that I can do all things through Christ who gives me strength. I know how to pray and trust God through it all. I have dignity because I understand that what I go through works together for my good. I can walk boldly before His throne of grace and receive forgiveness for my insufficiencies. I can forgive and not harness hate because I know how to release my pain. I can laugh at days to come because of the days that I left behind to fully trust and depend on Him. With Him…

You too can survive.

Mica Saunders

She is clothed in strength and dignity, and she laughs without fear of the future.

Anonymous

In November 2015, I was awakened by what I thought was the most devastating news I could ever receive. A phone call from the other woman asking if I was the other woman to a man that I dedicated a lot of my time and love to for more than 6 years. I was completely shocked and devastated and almost lost myself. After months of tears and confiding with friends and family, I would gradually find an outlet to give myself relief and determination when I begun to turn things around and use my pain to fuel a new-found passion for fitness. This would prove to be a life-changing chapter in my world…eventually.

    I recall it like it was yesterday. Mid-morning around 8am I was sitting on the couch eating breakfast and watching TV when my phone started to vibrate. I had a text coming in from a number that I didn't recognize asking me *"how did I know my boyfriend at the time?"*. As soon as I read the message my heart dropped. I text back *"who is this?"* The phone responds that she was his girlfriend along with her name. No more texting- I called the young lady, but she didn't answer. I was in a state of shock so my attention turned to talking to my mom. While we conversed, I received a call. She introduced herself and shared with me that the night before my (now newly minted former) boyfriend and she stayed at a hotel to celebrate his deployment. That morning when I had messaged him- she saw it. She wanted to know why was someone else other than her calling her boyfriend "baby". She told me that they met each other in November 2014 and three months later he asked her to be his girlfriend. Now there was complete silence on the phone. My mind was in the twilight zone and I was in a fog! She said she was sorry but I expressed to her don't be sorry, obviously you didn't know about me He knew what he was doing; he is the only one that needs to apologize. Shockingly, the young lady shared with me that my fresh-ex had a fling with a girl that works on the same ship with him. Unfortunately, she found a note from the other woman in his pocket when she washed his clothes for him one day. The guy that I knew became the guy he said he would never be. He was completely living a double-life.

In a handful of minutes, I was starring in my own *"Get Out"* movie, disappearing deep into my couch. I was in the 'sunken place'.

After finishing talks with the lady, I sent my fresh-ex a text to call me. Twenty minutes later, I calmly relayed that I spoke with his girlfriend. His response: sorrow, coupled with the explanation that he didn't know how to tell me. He said he got lonely and needed someone. Besides (here comes the reversal) it was hard for him to tell me because I am so emotional!!   Really?? EMOTIONAL??!!

I'm too emotional... that's why you couldn't tell me.

More first-class delivered excuses came in packages wrapped with: "There was never the right time to tell you" and "I didn't want to hurt you." Guess what you are doing right now? You are hurting me!!!

I asked him: Why did you do this to me? I thought we were going to get married one day.

I've been with you throughout your whole military career...How could you do me so wrong? I support you throughout your career? I traveled to every state you were stationed in.
I loved you! Did you really ever love me?
    Denial had set in!
    In the Denial phase, you are:

Desperate for answers!
Can't believe this is happening to you!
Saddled with irrational thoughts and behaviors.
Contradicting the breakup.
Swinging back and forth in between thoughts.
Can't accept that it's over!

All you can talk about is your break-up and how it has you confused, pained and disorganized.

Fast Forward

    After I finished speaking to fresh-ex, I got in the car and drove down to DC to see my friend in the hospital and her new baby. I felt like I had tunnel vision, my mind was in another dimension. My mind was totally spaced out. Thank God with I made it to DC without getting in an accident. I was in the room visiting… except I was there by not there. I kept thinking about how is this happening to me? Why is this happening? If only I had done things differently.

I apologize to my friend for my absence of mind; she understood my anguish.

Throughout the day I was still trying to process but later that evening around reality had set in and I had entered a safe space in my mind. Rehearsal for a church event was next on the evening agenda. No sooner than the coordinator asking how I was doing, a wall of internally vaulted pain cracked and I broke down crying in her arms. I had held my tears in for over 10 hours, and in that holy arena, God told me it was time to release them. My mind and body knew that I was in a safe space and I released all my frustration.

It's Coming Together Now

I started to replay our relationship in my head and everything started to come together. The signs are there in plain view but often we are not consciously aware of them until a big issue!

I knew that getting over this breakup was going to be hard but I knew with will power and determination I could do it.

When I had free time, I focused hard on not isolating myself. I surrounded myself daily around individuals that love me. The first holiday season was the toughest. They say idle time is the worst. To keep myself level I made sure I attended all my family events. Being around family made me feel so happy because initially as soon as I left I started thinking about the fresh-ex…

…again.

It would be almost a full year later before I <u>finally</u> faced my feelings. I didn't want to keep temporarily fixing the pain; I wanted to bury anguish forever. This final time, I decided to <u>really</u> focus on Micah; to feel every last residue of emotion from the beginning so that I wouldn't continue to face the same cycle of pain.

Time heals everything! Taking that time out to heal gave me a refreshed outlook on life. I started leaning on the word of GOD more. Daily I would think about my ex less, brushing off periodic thoughts and kept going on with my day. I used my idle time to study and build my business and even hired a business coach to accelerate my growth. I was in a new arena of living: setting goals I once thought I could never achieve. I started working out more and eating healthy, healing daily. I literally was watching my life transform and resurrect from the 'sunken place'. God was reshaping my life. Sometimes He has to put His red 'X' on things to let us know: 'That's not what He want for us."

GOD help me transform my life. Today, I aid other women who have experienced this same hurt, pain and feelings of depression and devastation.

I launched my program *Breakup2Shapeup* to guide women on how to get emotionally navigate a breakup or divorce through personal development and fitness.

My affirmation is now yours to have: *You're braver than you believe, stronger than you seem and smarter than you think.*

The Covering

Mone't Horton

For if ye live after the flesh, ye shall die: but if ye through the Spirit do mortify the deeds of the body, ye shall live. For as many as are led by the Spirit of God, they are the sons of God. For ye have not received the spirit of bondage again to fear; but ye have received the Spirit of adoption, whereby we cry, Abba, Father. The Spirit itself beareth witness with our spirit, that we are the children of God: And if children, then heirs; heirs of God, and joint-heirs with Christ; if so be that we suffer with him, that we may be also glorified together.

Romans 8:13-17

Growing up, my father, my dad was in the picture, but was not in the picture the way I desired him to be. I would always say, the girls with the girls and the boys with the boys. I was always hanging out with my mother and my brother was with my father. In my childhood, during my later elementary, early middle school year's, I believe, my mother and my father separated. That was a lot for me because while there was transition going on at home. I was transitioning to another age and grade level. While I was excited for going to the next grade, it was also all so terrifying.

Who would like me? Who would I hang out with? I was more conscious of my outfits…all those pressures that young people encounter when growing up began to hit me. My mom was always there to make sure I had all that I needed. And at the end of the day reinforced that I was beautiful and her big girl, so on and so forth. While my dad had a presence in my life, I honestly didn't get the paternal reinforcements that I thought I should be getting as a growing teenager.

He would always show up to pop his collar at graduations and celebrations, but he was not present during the major valley lows that I had to endure to get to the mountain tops of achievement. So much so, that as I grew older a void and sour spot grew in me towards my dad. I would still be cordial and hang out from time to time, but in the back of my mind and heart, I was like really? Are you serious? You have got to be kidding me…

I was never a disrespectful child. I learned to keep my feelings back within me until there were times of massive explosion. I kept it within. Which I know now was not healthy.

Into my high school years and college, the cycle of showing up when it was time to celebrate continued. There were always excuses of why he couldn't help with this or that and I was just totally fed up...
My mother shared my grief. Even as I sit here and type these words, I can recall and feel the emotions that I felt in those moments well up in me. It was a hard time in my life. Don't get me wrong my father took care of the responsibilities of the household, but there were pockets of paternal voids that had been sprinkled throughout my life that had created within me a hardened heart towards my father.
I am still talking about moving from your REALITY to your WEALTHY PLACE. See this was my reality. Into my college years, I struggled with this hardened heart. I went to church, continued with my life because it had to go on, but again, I had this hardened heart.

I had not realized at the time, but it impacted my relationships with the males in my life. Trust issues and not being able to take them for what they said they would do. After all, I had been let down so many times from the one person, the 1st male that I ever encountered—my father. I had feelings of not being enough—I'm short, I am overweight, I am this and that—simply put, not enough. Yes, these are feelings that I faced and of course life was still going on...

I never, ever had realized how much that hardened heart towards my dad had impacted my relationships with the opposite sex. I grew up in a family of beautiful, independent women who were confident in their own skin and did not wait for a man, at least as far as I could see to do anything for them. So, this was my experience, what I knew to be my REALITY—so I followed suit. I was not arrogant or prideful, but I was truly independent.

****

One day, during my college year's I was at my grandfather's house, packing up some items and God convicted me right on the spot! I had been reading my spiritual aunt, Annette E. Morton's book, *"Transference of Coverings—understanding the Role of a Man Over a Woman's Life."* As the title hints, the book brought to light the key roles, responsibilities a man has in a woman's life and their significance. In reading, I instantly had to confront the void of a close and authentic relationship with my father. Yes, I was blessed to have male figures in my life at church, school and at other points leading up to that moment, BUT I longed to have such a relationship with my birth father. I was totally thankful for the support of those men, but it never could fill that void.
The truth is that as I got older, took care of my business and attempted to burry my feelings, hurt and pain my hardened heart was growing too. It was not getting better, at all. As I continued to read the book, I was faced with this REALITY and knew that I had to yet again, con front it head-on. That day in my grandfather's house, was the day that God took the cap off my pain and gave me a RELEASE. The one that I longed for…
I was in the bathroom, looking in the mirror and tears begin to flood my face. I wept and I wept. I literally

felt that with every tear God was draining me of all the toxins that advanced my hardened heart over the years.

First, as I stood there looking in the mirror, I had to **confront my REAL feelings**—no more denial, no more hiding, no more faking the funk on how I felt about my father. If I was truly saved and God was going to use me beyond my wildest dreams, I had to get over "this." It became less and less about my father, it was more and more about MY relationship with God and what He was doing, wanted to do and would do through me. I had to accept my father as a human being. Yes, he is human too. I had always pictured that a father had super powers and did super things, that he would be MY superman—and come down to save me from harm, wipe the tears from my eyes and be the first example of what a man should be in my life and how he should treat me. Well, that is not what I ever felt and in that moment, I had to dismantle the pedal stool that I had placed my father on.

Secondly, I had to **BE OK** with it. Be OK with the fact that my father was human and had faults, after all, we all do… that was not all, the other side of that is that his actions was a result of his experiences and exposure.

Lastly, in accepting and being OK with those truths, I had to then **manage my expectations**. For me, this was achieved by not expecting him to do any more or less than what he had been doing. In this realization, I gained so much strength and power over my hardened heart I buried for so long. My hardened heart was NO MORE. God had come in that moment and RELEASED me of the overwhelming pressure and burdens I had carried. It was not easy, but from that day to date, I have taken steps towards embracing my father for who he is and I have witnessed God during the rest in shaping and molding him to the man He wants him to be.

Shakira Johnson

I praise you because I am fearfully and wonderfully made; your works are wonderful, I know that full well.

Psalm 139:14

    From a very young age I have always been highly driven. For many years I fought through the mental road blocks that hindered me from seeing myself as the Queen I was always meant to be. I battled with various issues such as: low self–esteem, depression, people-pleasing and self-consciousness. Satan who is our enemy is a tricky fool; he will tell you a lie, convince you that it is true and even use the people you love most to say all kinds of hurtful things to you and against you. The lie starts out as a tiny thought planted in our minds like a seed, for example "You know you are not successful because you have not achieved…xyz." Eventually, you will begin to ponder on it and then you'll start to speak it. These words soon begin to spread like wildfire and loved ones are constantly reminding you of what you have not done. Situations like this will cause you to make unnecessary evaluations, measuring your success in comparison to others. For some, these are just thoughts, but for me these were countless events and scenarios that clouded my mind and caused to me feel worthless and rejected.

So there I was living as if I had something to prove because I was wrestling with the thoughts and often replaying those words which had followed me into adulthood. Fighting in the flesh, different spirits that had made themselves comfortable and had no plans of leaving.

As an adolescent, I was saved, attended church and loved Christ, but somehow I had not overcome those thoughts and feelings. I had close relatives who literally destroyed my self-esteem. Mental and substance abuse ran rampant throughout generations on both sides of my family. Satan gets on my last nerve. When I think about it, he has basically told me the same tired lie all my life just in diverse ways. "You will never be anything," "You are a failure," "You aren't good enough," "He will never love you." If you are told something long enough, you eventually begin to believe it. I do not know about you, but I am sick and tired of the lies! If you are not sick and tired of the lies…GET SICK AND TIRED! Pick up that Crown and remind yourselves about what God's word says about whom you were created to be. Often, you will need to find an outlet because we are physical beings and these spiritual battles have their effects on our bodies. Stress is NOT of God. You will need to find ways to release these feelings so that God can restore you in ways unimaginable.

As a teen, journaling and writing poetry and songs helped me to cope. Truthfully, my poetry was dark and emotional but it painted a vivid picture of how I felt. I was able to share one of my poems with my mom when I was 14 years old. It brought her to tears because she had no idea that all of those things were flooding my mind. That was the first step on my journey to healing. Queens, what are some of your hobbies? Whatever they may be, I encourage you to enjoy them often.

Currently, worship is my weapon of mass destruction and it is yours! Use it as often as you need to, because you deserve to live a life free of rejection and any of its attachments.

Queens, God is with you always he was there when you were conceived and will be there throughout every stage of this journey. God often reminds us that we are not alone, this battle is spiritual and He is fighting on our behalf. God's word prevails over any lie the enemy can ever spew out.

Reflection: *Think of a time when the enemy may have used someone close to you to say something hurtful or demeaning about you.*

_____
_____
_____
_____
_____

Scripture References: Jeremiah 1:5, Jeremiah 29:11, 1 Peter 2:9

What are some ways that you can free your mind from all of the clutter that is causing you to feel defeated, rejected, unwanted or misused?

_____
_____
_____
_____
_____

Reject: to refuse to accept, to cast off

I met my father at age five for the first time and had only seen him a few times after. I could never understand how my father could live within minutes from me yet never make any attempt to be active in my life. Many questions filled my head, no answers were ever offered. I remember thinking if ever given the opportunity, I'd share with him all of my talents and accomplishments throughout school. I wanted him to be proud- and involved. I needed him to love me enough to come around and teach me the things that my mom couldn't. I longed to experience what his love was like. I had many thoughts and feelings, mostly emptiness because my father lived down the street and with one of my siblings; but from me he remained distant. I remember thinking *"how could he live so close but be so far away?" "What made my siblings more special?"* They saw him more often; spent more time and made lifelong memories with him. They shared a special bond with our father, one that I had always wanted yet never had. When I was eight years old my father was incarcerated, his learning of me consisted of what I shared via letters I sent. We wrote one another and I visited him a few times but nothing could ever replace the feelings that lay deep inside. No letter or visit could dispel the fact that he made his choices-and I wasn't one of them. I will never say that he did not love me, but his actions and decisions made it hard to tell. At age 16 my father was released from prison, that Thanksgiving and Christmas we were able to spend time together and made memories that will forever be etched in my heart.

After the holidays, I had not heard from my father. He had begun working a new job and was expecting a new baby. I remember not hearing from him on my birthday and being disappointed yet again. I became frustrated with him and was at a point where I no longer wanted to deal with him however, on this one particular day he called to see how I was doing. While on the phone I had an opportunity to tell him just how I felt. I shared with him how hurt I was that he had never truly been an active part of my life and how disappointed I was that he didn't call me for my birthday especially since this was the first year he was home from prison. During this phone conversation, my father asked if he could visit me. That same day, he came to visit me we ate dinner and I remember finding the folder that I had kept just for him. This folder was filled with certificates, awards, photos, etc. My father stayed for a few hours and I was finally able to share with him my achievements. That day had turned into one of the best days I had ever shared with my father. The very next day I received a call at work. By this time, I was 17 years old. The call was from my relatives telling me that my father had been killed in a hit and run accident. He died instantly, and that was all of the information that they could share.

It has been over a decade since my father has been gone from this earth and I still struggle with the fact that he is not here with me. Queens, when I tell you that God has designed us to experience life and He teaches us to forgive those who have hurt us in the process. I had no clue that this would be our last time together. I am grateful for the time that was shared, even if it was only for a short amount of time.

Reveal: to make (something secret or hidden) publicly or generally known

Queen, are you battling with unforgiveness? Harboring feelings of bitterness? I encourage you to channel those hidden places deep in your heart that we tend to overlook, cover up and even run away from. Take a moment to think about if there is anyone who you may not have forgiven, if there are any situations that you just cannot seem to get over, reveal them and present them before the Lord.

_____
_____
_____
_____

So, since we are revealing some things, there is one more piece of this story I would like to share with you. This, by far, has been the hardest thing for me to reveal to anyone. Just a couple of years after my father passed away I began dating. Something inside of me knew that I should take my time but I had always longed for security and for a man to love and accept me. Now, I know that I was young, but I had always dreamed of finding that perfect man, living a successful life and achieving many common goals. As cliché as it may be, this was my dream. In all honesty no relationship is ever perfect especially when you are young, but with this particular relationship there was something different. I grew to fall in love with him, he loved me I could tell, he supported me and truly this was the ideal relationship…the one that I had always wanted. We spent several years of our lives together and I just knew that he was the one for me except, I was not the one for him. Queens, I asked you to reveal those deep hidden places for a reason you see when certain issues get buried long enough they eventually become invisible until you literally forget that they were ever there. I had buried all of those feelings of rejection, low self-esteem, bitterness and anger so deep that I had convinced myself that I was healed NOPE! I was very much still broken, still bitter and still an ugly fragile mess deep down inside. Have you ever heard the phrase "Hurt people, Hurt People" well I know firsthand.

I began to belittle to him, to verbally attack him and even physically lashed out at him. There I was with someone I loved, someone who loved me but I was so broken and bitter from the failed relationships with family, exes, friends, etc. that I was no good to him or anyone else for that matter. We decided to break up and to hurt him even more I changed my number and cut off all contact with him for a few months. During that time I realized what I had and wanted desperately to try again. I could not see us spending all of this time together just to let it all go. In the end we got back together but this time he was different, He was my man but he was more distant more focused on other things and more determined not to allow me to attack his pride. Who could blame him? But this time around I was deeply in love, I knew that he was the one and I didn't want to do anything to ruin us. He became so distant: were we even still together? We talked about marriage, but a wedding was nowhere in sight. We continued spending time with each other, fortifying false hopes. During our conversations he avoided questions about the future of our relationship and why we couldn't be together in union. I would lash out and although it was not physical in any way it would have a lasting impact on both of us. He eventually connected with someone else, and ending our relationship completely. When I questioned him, his reply sliced my existence: "I needed someone on my level and with a Degree." He knew that these choice cocktail of words would pain me. Here I am with no degree, still in community college and no longer good enough for him; he had moved on. The hurt never left me. As I tried to move on he played a dangerous game with me keeping me around in one form or another playing yo-yo with my feelings. I wanted answers, and details. I wanted to know just what his relationship was with this other woman and if I even still had a chance.

    Queens, I learned a harsh lesson that year. If

God says No, Let him Go! Some relationships are blessings while others are lessons. In this case my lesson was that you cannot build a house with missing pieces.

Release: to relieve from something that confines, burdens, or oppresses

For far too long Satan has stolen your hope, dreams and desires. He has literally tried to kill your faith and destroy your self-awareness. Queen, the devil has lied to you long enough You are Chosen, You are Valuable and You are living in God's purpose for your life. No matter what your issues may be allow the Lord to restore you and command the enemy to return every single thing he has stolen. Queens, I pray that you have been blessed and I encourage you to release whatever it is unto the Lord so that you can build your family, ministry and business because "You are an Original Designed and Chosen by God"

In conclusion, if you intend to live life the way that God has created you to live you will need to be restored. This is a deep down cleansing that can only come from him.

Shawan Pettie

Every little girl should grow up believing she is a PRINCESS, so that when she becomes a woman, she won't struggle with being a QUEEN.

Shawan Pettie

Have you ever repeatedly received compliments and the best you can return is a blank stare until you can muster up a "thank you" as you try to figure out who they are talking about? I surely have. I must admit, when I look at my life today, I have much to be grateful for. I have a successful career in government, a professional speaker and etiquette consultant clientele base. I own my own home, drive a nice car and I'm in ministry. I even earned a First Runner Up placing in a beauty pageant. In the many circles that I am a part of, I'm often admired and sought after as a mentor and a woman that other women either want to be like or be around. However, at the end of the day when I drive home in that nice car, open the door, greet my dog, kick off my shoes and take off my makeup, it's just ME. There is no one telling me how great I am or what an amazing job I did. I sit in my living room and the fight against all of the negative things that I've heard throughout my childhood and young adulthood begins. I find myself trying to drown out all of the voices that I heard from bullies and sometimes even family, so that I can truly believe the wonderful things that people say. People can often see the greatness in us before we see it in ourselves. When people looked at me, they saw my crown, but because I had never grown accustomed to wearing my tiara as a little girl, a full crown and the compliments that came along with it were uncomfortable to me. My identity as a princess and someone worthy of love had been stolen and I never knew I was royalty.

    I remember it like it was yesterday, my first day of pre-school! My mother, like most do, dropped me off at school, and I was ready to make new friends! Except, these young children weren't so friendly. The staff at the school wasn't friendly either. I didn't like pre-school and the thought of going to school every day threw me into an emotional tizzy. I would have crying fits, to the point of vomiting. And it was then that I experienced my first bullying episode. I was officially dubbed "the spit-up girl." The children would tease me every day and it almost became a self-fulfilling prophecy because I would cry and throw up. Can you believe it? Eventually, graduation day came and I thought to myself, "Yes! New school, no more bullies!" Little did I know, I would experience bullying on through 9th grade. I was called fat, ugly and stinky. I wore hand me down clothes and my mom prided herself on not dressing me in "fads." Instead of the latest "Cross Colors" jeans, I would get dresses and suits for church. What I wouldn't give to get clothes for school so that I could be cool like the other kids. I felt like I never fit in. However, it was this time of isolation caused by the bullying that caused me to become closer to God. My relationship with God was very close for someone my age. While others were playing during recess and I was inside because I was the last to get picked for any sport or game, I remember sitting in the corner and just singing hymns to God; hymns like "What a Friend We Have in Jesus" and "It is Well With My Soul." I guess you could say I developed a spiritual maturity way before my time.

Proverbs 4:23 admonishes us to "Above all else,

guard your heart, for everything you do flows from it (NIV)." If you grew up in church like me, you've heard people tell you a thousand times to "guard your heart." And if you didn't grow up in church and are hearing this phrase for the first time don't worry, you're in the same boat with many who heard this phrase growing up in church because almost NO ONE tells you what this means or how to do it…LOL! Think of your heart as the place that houses your identity, thoughts, and emotions (HOME). Your greatest defense (FENCE) against potential threats are a great sense of self-worth and self-esteem. When you were born, God deposited everything you needed to be uniquely who you are. You are fearless, you love freely and your personality begins to shine through without anyone telling you how. You have to just BE. Well, negative words from others, emotional abuse, people who try to re-define who you are, and lack of acceptance and affirmation, begins to tear down that fence of self-worth and self-esteem. Now, you have nothing to guard you against the threats that come to steal your identity. Those threats come in the form of people and circumstances. You become vulnerable. At this point, you need to summon an emergency team to repair and rebuild your self-worth, self-esteem, and identity. This reconstruction can be unique to each individual, in terms of time and method, but for me, with the help of God, loved ones, and a commitment to be an active participant in my own mental and emotional health, I have begun to rebuild my fence and reclaim my identity as royalty, and you can too.

I know what it's like to feel alone. I've felt alone most of my life (and still do at times), and yet, God found ways to let me know that He was always there for me. I'm grateful for the relationship that I developed with Christ because, without it, I can honestly say that I don't think that I would be alive to write this to you today. I remember crying myself to sleep almost every night for YEARS and feeling the comfort of God lulling me to sleep. I began studying the Bible as a youth and finding scriptures that talked about how much God loves me, who He created me to be and His promises towards me. One thing's for sure, when God makes a promise, you can expect Him to keep it. If you haven't already done so, study the Bible regarding who God says you are. Write it down and put it in places that you can see. Re-visit it often. It truly does work. Such a strong faith came in handy in those moments I felt the hopelessness and depression clouds overshadow me to the point of suicidal ideation. Every moment that I considered taking my own life, I paused and thought about the hope that I have in Jesus and faith that tomorrow could always be better. The truth of the matter is that if you end your life today, you will never know. That's the trick of the enemy as it pertains to hopelessness and suicide. If he can get you to end your life today, you will never have the opportunity to embrace the hope that the dawn can bring. God has promised to grant us new mercies with each morning. Unless we possess the ability to know what each day will bring and the ultimate end of our story (which we don't), we have absolutely no way of knowing that things WON'T get better. Think of it this way. Our life is a story...just one giant narrative. The author of our life narrative is God. He and He alone knows the protagonists, antagonists, and plot. He knows the conclusion before He writes the introduction. Each day of our lives is a turn of the page. When we contemplate suicide, we are saying that we are willing to take the pen out of the hand of the Author and rip out the pages of the rest of the book. I was there before. I've been there many times. The torture of hopelessness overtook me to the point where I wanted to discontinue my story. Yet, everytime I considered it, I wondered what the end was going to be. The only way for me to be able to find out was to keep turning the page! If you are reading this and feel like you can't take it anymore, please don't give up! I'm only asking you to do one thing each day and, moment by moment for some, and that is, keep turning the page. You will find that as you keep turning, there are some unexpected plot twists that God will have in store for you! Don't end your story prematurely.

    My challenges with my identity continued on through young adulthood. Because my fence had many holes in it, I found myself going from one unhealthy relationship to the next. My choice in men was not the best. The vulnerability that comes with not knowing who you are puts you at risk for wolves to enter through the gaps and take advantage of your weaknesses. I made poor decisions regarding interactions with men, which led to me having been sexually harassed and date raped on at least three separate occasions. I reported none of them. Date rape is tricky because I often would blame myself for being flirtatious and playing with fire. "If only I hadn't gone to that guy's house that night." "If only I hadn't worn that outfit." "If only I hadn't engaged in activities that naturally led to sex." The thoughts continue to weigh on you until you tell yourself that you deserved what you got. The truth of the matter is that NO woman deserves to be violated in any way. The act is heinous and the onus is on the violator. However, I will say this. Ladies, when you know your worth, you will not go searching for validation from men. It will help keep you out of situations that could have possibly been avoided.

Then, there's emotional rape. For me, this rape took place when a man saw my vulnerability and craftily entered through the gaps in my heart. One of the most regrettable things that I've experienced is allowing a married man to get through. When the relationship started out, he approached me like a mentor, a brother, a confidant. He wanted to fix the broken pieces in my life. He wanted to be to me what all the other men were not. Again, when you are in a place of vulnerability, your defenses are not as strong as they once were and your ability to recognize wolves can be very dull. This took place after I had been raped and mistreated by several different men. This relationship continued for years until one day, he became sexual and inappropriate in his interactions. I tried to fight it for years, I mean years, however, as I was hurt more and more by others and as the emotions grew, I had no more fight left in me. No matter what I do, I cannot take this back, however, as I grew in an understanding of who I was, I was able to completely end the relationship and move forward. I have regrets, but I have peace. I understand why it happened and now I simply desire to help other women not fall prey to the same thing that I did. Don't ever get to the point where you have fallen so out of love with yourself that you allow someone to compromise your values and who you are. They thrive off of your silence because they believe you won't tell anyone because of your own culpability. Repent and break the silence, and walk in the peace that comes from knowing that God is able and just to forgive. Moreover, please, please, forgive yourself my sister. It is imperative for your healing.

  Claiming back my identity in spite of these experiences truly did require a team-effort, however, I too had to be part of the team, just like you will need to be for your own victory. Take the time to invest in your emotional reconstruction through reading material that will build you up. In addition to the Bible, some of the best books I've read were, "Safe

People: How to Find Relationships that are Good for You and Avoid Those that Aren't," by Dr. Henry Cloud and Dr. John Townsend; "Sex and the Soul of a Woman," by Paula Rinehart; and "Addicted to Counterfeit Love," by Dr. Vikki Johnson. I also worked with a therapist during my journey and took anti-depressants as part of my treatment for my depression. I have no regrets and am so glad that I prayerfully sought out professional help to expedite my healing process. Faith and science are not mortal enemies. In fact, when God is in the midst, the two can come together in beautiful harmony. Lastly, after learning the difference between safe people and unsafe people, build your accountability community. Positive relationships and affirmations are integral to the healing process. They help you to balance your confidence scale and replace the negativity that you have begun to clear out.

Your story might not be exactly like my story, but know that once you are sure of who you are and stand in the posture of victory, no one can easily come in and take it from you. You will begin to find that there were certain blessings that you could not have or opportunities that you could not enter into until you knew who you were in your heart. From this place, as Proverbs 4:23 states, EVERYTHING YOU DO FLOWS. This is why it is the first place of attack. Not knowing who you are paralyzes you and keeps you from entering the place of abundance that God has in store for you. So, my dear sisters, please continue to guard your heart, recognize your royal posture, and if you have experienced a breakdown in your defenses, immediately begin reconstruction like your life depends on it, because it does. Your crown is waiting for you.

Temica Gross

Whether you think you can or whether you think you can't, you're right.

Henry Ford

As a business coach, author, speaker, a mompreneur and a mentor it's sometimes unreal to hear other people describe my recent accomplishments when delivering my introduction. Consciously, I am aware that I have a lot of successes to be thankful for and I'm grateful for every step of elevation in the process. However I could never forget that moment in time when my life stood still and fear, doubt and shame controlled my very being. I'm speaking of those moments long before I experienced my breakthrough and my accomplishments began to pour in. That moment in life when I couldn't see past my current situation and firmly believed that nothing would improve my current situation unless I won the lottery, lost 80lbs, married Idris Elba and moved to England. I often describe this moment in my life as my 'bottom' because it's the point where I truly believed nothing could get any worse and I was forced to make a decision. A decision to wallow in self-pity and surround myself in the comforts of defeat or to arm myself with positive affirmations and defeat my own self-doubt. If you're reading this book, it's safe to say that I chose the latter, but now I share with you *how* I recognized the emotional 'hole' I had dug for myself- and how I finally put the shovel down.

"How did I end up here?" I mumbled through my sobs. "This is NOT supposed to be my life!" I yelled, sitting on the floor of my tiny fairly-empty apartment. My trembling voice echoed and bounced off shaded white walls. My back rests against the seat of my newly purchased Wal-Mart special sofa as I cupped my head in my hands while staring at the floor. My semi-furnished apartment looked identical to your average freshman's college dorm room minus the red lava lamp. I was surrounded by silence which for me was unusual, I was used to my then four-year-old running circles around my every step. I won't get to hear those footsteps and childish giggles for another three days. This is my husband's weekend to spend time with our son, but it also happens to be our first weekend apart as separated spouses.

"You can do this Meek" I whispered.

"You can start over again; you can rebuild". I sat on the floor a while longer still quietly coaching myself.

"Come on Meek, you've got this."

I continued to repeat mantra of positive words; however, they eventually held no weight for me. As if they weren't true and were just a few hollow syllables just dancing on my tongue and I'd find myself crying out all over again until I felt lifeless.

With each passing day since I saw my 'bottom' I felt paralyzed by fear of the unknown. "What will happen to me if…?" "How will I support my son and myself financially?" I was in a constant state of worry and the mental questions would just keep coming. "Will my son think I'm a bad parent?" "What if I can't provide him with all the finer things in life?". Question after question after question! I found myself slowly slipping into a mild state of depression. I would hide my fears from my friends, family and coworkers and wear the biggest brightest and phoniest smile on my face to not cause alarm or alert anyone to what I was really experiencing. Little

did I know then I was doing more harm than good to myself by not seeking help to navigate the troubled waters. But I was so afraid of this unknown fate that I believed my fear would eventually kill me. You see my
'bottom' had the power to steal my breath at any given moment. I can remember having trouble breathing just thinking about a much worse scenario. I would experience heart palpitations at least 10 times a day: at work, in the car, at the grocery store- virtually everywhere. Imagine what it feels like to think you're having a heart attack because you're in a constant state of fear? Now imagine a fresh wave of fear sweeping over you when thinking of what will happen to your toddler and family because you decided it was time to end it all? It's been said that, "Heavy is the head that wears the crown…". My depressive state manifested because of my lack of ability to recognize my Queenly power. I didn't know that then or I would have surely stood tall in my full authority and command my treacherous state of thinking to perish. Instead, I continued to suffer in silence, hoping that one day… something magical would happen and my 'bottom' would just vanish.

Months had passed since I became submissive and accustomed to throwing my own private pity parties several times a month. My own sad personal party that included red wine and a few good episodes of Good Times and Sanford and Son. Once, I remember sitting on the couch and getting a clear image of myself on a stage speaking and empowering a crowd of women. I was singing and dancing to Diana Ross's hit song, "I'm Coming Out". Then it was gone. Have you ever been given a glimpse of your future but because of your present state, you immediately kill the vision? That was me, except I repeatedly assassinated my dream! I began to see images of myself in magazines, autographing books and being interviewed by popular influencers such as Oprah… and would laugh it off and blame it on the wine. Encourage and motivate someone else? Me? Share a stage with a top influencer and receive recognition? Me? Little ol' Temica who grew up in the housing projects of 'the Bronx? What I failed to realize then was, the 'how' should never have been my concern. I needed to take concentrated steps towards that goal and it WOULD manifest.

One night after paying every bill due that month, my bank account held just enough to fill my tank with gas for the upcoming week. Frustrated and embarrassed that I didn't even have enough to take my son to Chuck e Cheese, I felt my body going limp and a good pity party cry getting ready to begin. Anger swept over me and instead of simply crying in shame I cried out loud, "What do I need to do to live in my abundance?!" Have you ever asked for something out loud and received and instant reply? A reply so clear you wondered if there was someone in the next room listening in on your conversation waiting to deliver the promise. Well, I'd like to think that in that moment, the universe gave me exactly what I asked for because in the furthest corner of my heavy heart, I began to feel a growing surge of energy. An energy that would ignite a fire, spark desire and recharge my power. It was as if every positive attribute I possessed suddenly rushed to my mind and reminded me that I was and will always be a Queen. Every triumph, victory and every personal success story began to play out in my mind one by one. I saw myself in a new, bigger and brighter light. On that night, I repositioned my crown.

Other than an occasional sniffle here and there, the room was still quiet. Except for the internal conversation I was having. Eyes closed, I felt myself nodding my head in agreement to make a change to my current situation beginning that night. Encouragement and explanation were flooding me, unpacking all the reasons why I needed to get it together and to tap into my true gift so that I could reign in my personal "Queendom". I realized in that moment that my "bottom" wasn't really my "bottom". Everything that I was afraid of and made me shutter in fear and terror night after night, week after week and month after month was actually my new BEGINNING! That unknown shadowy entity that I had been ducking and dodging all this time was nothing more than a light fog that was protecting the vision of my abundance until I was ready to receive it and believe it.

Deciding to finally climb out of the hole and

remembering my power wasn't easy. Now I needed to trust a new process. But since I doubted my ability to become my own rescue for so long, believing in my capabilities was challenging. It was going to take concentrated and forceful actions to build up my positive stamina.

Remembering my vision of autographing books, I began to work on my first book that month. I worked with a coach, researched the industry, sacrificed sleep and burned the midnight oil plenty of times and even used my lunch breaks at work to do something, anything related to me completing my book. Three short months later I birth my first book titled, *"Live Victoriously – 4 East Steps to Defeating Self-Doubt"* and topped the charts making me an Amazon.com bestselling author. Me? A bestselling author? You bet! A focused three months will make you face your fears and forget about the 'how'.

I continued to make progressive strides that aligned with my visions. I began the roots of networking with intention to creating my own entrepreneur group, *Tenacious Tribe*. Now I was supporting and educating new entrepreneurs in various areas of their entrepreneurial journey. I also hosted my first sold-out women's empowerment conference! My venue was jam packed with so many beautiful and purpose driven women that wanted to make an incredible shift in their lives. I can remember standing in the hall before I was to be introduced praying with my sister and saying, "I just want to be effective" and as I heard my biography being read it was then that I realized, I already had been.

Queen: I don't know where you are in life at this moment. I don't know what may be weighing you down or what may be clouding your vision but I do know it can't beat you [if you don't let it]. You were creatively designed to complete an amazing mission but you won't be able to see it through until you raise your head, grab hold of your scepter and stand in your full power. It will look scary in the beginning and you may doubt yourself over and over again, but you have to stay the course to reap the reward of living in your abundance. Now take a deep breath; find that inner strength and prepare yourself for what I'm sure will be the beginning of a beautiful adventure.

You were made for this!

From Concrete to Crown

Violesia Tull

For I know the plans I have for you, declares the LORD, plans to prosper you and not to harm you, plans to give you hope and a future.

Jeremiah 29:11

Hey, my name is Violesia Tull, and well here's a little about me. I'm a mother of three beautiful children. I grew up in the inner city of Baltimore, and was sexually abused from the ages of 5 - 14 years old by 7 men, was introduced to pornography at 7 yrs old, idolized the corner life, and held my first gun at 8 years old. It was rough growing up on the blocks of Park Heights, Spring Hill and Poplar Grove. I imagined living in this beautiful neighborhood, where being molested every day wasn't normal. I knew my life would be greater than my current situation. Getting there was going to be the challenge. I dropped out of high school right at my 12th year. That failure took a toll on me. I just knew I was going to be this business professional. I was wearing suits in high school. Even landed a few business deals with my high school Northwestern and Pimlico Race Tracks making badge buttons with their logo. I went back to school to Baltimore City College to get my diploma. They had a program that allowed you to get the remainder of your credits needed to get your High School diploma. I went on to college and it wasn't enough. I still felt like a failure with no direction. Taking the advice of people telling me what they think I should be or do. I pray that my short stories compels you to get up no matter how many times you fall!

Blacker than Dirt

It was a beautiful sunny day and my aunt lived across the street from me. Actually, it was like our family owned that block. That's how deep we were with the presence of my family on that block. No matter how mad we got at each other, no one else was allowed to mess with us. My family was so crazy. I was scared at times for the person who would mess with me. I was sometimes afraid to tell my brother or sister when I was being bullied. Okay, back to the aunty. She invited the cousins over to play. I think I was around six or seven years old. It was a birthday celebration. All you could hear was water splashing and laughter. Aunty had some food cooking on the grill and the music, or should I say "oldies but goodies" jamming from the kitchen window. That was the life and you couldn't tell me it wasn't! Before I knew it everything shifted! Without warning a dark cloud immediately rushed over me. I knew immediately it was generational spirits coming for the sins of my father and generations before me. Before I could blink my eyes the fun turned into my face being thrust into the water of the pool. The thoughts in my mind began to race and my body began to lock up and tears started to form but the water from them dunking me replaced them. I couldn't believe that this was happening. Something welled up in me and I began fighting for my life. I thought , "Why are they doing this to me? God please help! " During that time I didn't even know there was a God. I'd heard my family speak about him casually in conversation or saying the name Jesus after a cussing match! And I would get all dressed up fancy for that season that comes once a year called Easter. I fought between saving my breath or screaming for help. Every time they pulled my head out the water by my hair I screamed HELP with all my might! And I still felt the scream wasn't good enough. I don't how I did it! Six people to my one. But somehow I broke from their grip! I ran so fast and so hard you would've thought I was in a marathon. I was screaming help! Help! Help! But they're screams and cheering while chasing me muted my cries for help. I was scared. I knew my life wasn't going to end this way. But I couldn't understand why my own family would put me through this. At that moment I thought of giving up. I almost gave up on me and on who I was to them. I felt meaningless like my family had no problem treating me like trash. I was devastated that day. Especially when they caught up with me. This God I'd only heard of failed me, like everyone else. Who will save me now? As mud filled my mouth and covered my whole body. I stopped twisting and turning to somehow break free. I gave up! They got back to the pool and proceeded with drowning me .And when they pulled my face up. I looked over to the house of my aunty and I saw her in the window. I locked eyes with her! My strength to scream was gone. I begged her with my eyes to help me, and she slowly turned her back towards me. At that moment I don't know where my strength came from, but God heard my cry and somehow I broke away.

I Must Not Matter

He had the opportunity to write his words of influence on my life like I'm writing on this paper. Instead he choose to kill me with his absence. Why would his life have any relevance in my journey? He became just another man who had "Failed me". With all the things that a man could offer. All I wanted was his love, his belief in me would've given me the hope that I can do anything. And I needed his protection. His abuse stripped me down like a newborn baby. Helpless! My self-defenses were weak. "Just shut up, keep quiet, and let him get it over with," I would say in the closet of my thoughts. I hated him! I think I even plotted a few times to murder him. I wanted him in those moments to experience the death he had caused me. For every time he called me dumb, for every slap his hands put to my face, and every time he inappropriately kissed my lips. For the times I had to massage his body, prepare his lunches for work, play the mistress in his secret life and iron his clothes.

I never understood why he hated me. I guess I felt because I never heard him say I love you. Maybe he did say it and I just missed it under all the noise from his yelling. I remember him fighting on his women. I remember sitting in the bathroom at his home and doing my little sister's hair and before I knew, his hand went across my face as if I were a stranger in the street. I fought back every tear that I wanted to let fall down my cheek. I'd seen him hit a woman, but never thought he would hit me that way.

I will never be able to answer why this man refused to be in my life or why any of this happened. All I know is that God has yet to fail me. He promised that when your father or mother forsakes you, He will take care of you. For so long I blamed myself for his lack of involvement in my life, but I have since concluded that we all have work to do on ourselves and he hasn't come to the point of change. I allowed someone else's shortcomings and faults to determine how I felt about myself. However, I have since learned the lesson that you are more than enough. You are full of purpose, promise and possibility! And if a person can't value that in you, then they are really not for you no matter their title.

I Wasn't Ready for This

Somehow I found myself searching for that lost part of me. I always knew that something was missing. I was angry with no hope. I had become lifeless. I knew I had been robbed of something meaningful but I hadn't determined how to get it back. Instead, I made the decision that I'd be the one to say who I gave myself to from now on. I would no longer be the victim or let him be my abuser. I was finally making the connection that my decisions were being affected by the abuse, lies, and neglect that I'd experienced.

A prince charming. The ghetto Park Heights version. There was absolutely nothing intriguing about this dude other than his good looks and slangish-English. And then I got a little closer, using him to quench a thirst that he couldn't fill because he was just as empty as I was. I realized his feet stank horribly because he didn't wear socks. He was as messed up of a soul as myself. He was no prince charming, we were both just human. I knew he wasn't the one, but I settled thinking he saw something special in me that I couldn't see in myself. I gave him my body and in return I felt every fiber of the heart close up. I slowly dried up from the inside out. Like a man in the desert searching for water because all he wants is something to quench his thirst. Like that man I died that day. I helplessly picked up the pieces of me that I squandered away. Walked to the bus stop with tears streaming down my cheeks and at that moment I cried out to a God I had neglected. I felt I'd again lost something I couldn't get back and had become a checkmark on another young man's list.

I don't know what it was about me, constantly being told I was an ugly black girl. I wasn't big on trying to fit in coming up. I was somewhat afraid of allowing people to get close. I think that came from all the hell I had been through while developing from a toddler into my preteens. But I will say I wanted someone to accept and notice me. I couldn't understand why everywhere I went a man was touching me, wanting to fight me, or putting me down. That wasn't the attention I wanted. It was like I'd been cursed and I hadn't gotten the memo.

Misplaced & Unidentified

I was like skeleton and bones. I felt like a rotten prune. Depression and suicide attempts had drained me. I lost all sense of who I was due to me never having the chance to develop. I found myself on the side of the road. Sitting in the gutter after trying to drink my sorrows away. So who I am? And who are you I ask? How do you allow yourself to become a person you were never acquainted with. What are your likes and dislikes? If you weren't broken and disappointed in life would you really be in that relationship? Most of the time we get comfortable with not fighting and using the authority placed within to take back or regain what was lost. For example our innocence. That inward feeling that you can conquer the world with that childlike faith.

I've always felt misplaced because we moved around so much. I would wake up expecting to be one place and remember that I was somewhere completely different. Every day to me was a war zone and I spent my moments in the prison of my mind while others around me were living. I had to watch out for explosives at every turn. I never knew who I was and I hated the person looking back at me from the mirror. Each of has the quiet voice within pushing and encouraging you to be the greater you. You mustn't give up! My memories from my childhood were nothing more than being a slave. A slave to men who made my purpose serving them. And that's what I carried into the beginning of my journey. But I have begun to find the woman of God that He created and meant in life. In the world wind of my storm, loss, and defeat Jesus found me and I found him.

Afia Yeboah

International Volunteer, Motivational Speaker, Fashion Model, and Community Leader, Afia acknowledges that her challenging yet village-like upbringing in Baltimore City inspired her to be a social agent of positive change. After attending the reputable Baltimore Polytechnic Institute, she received her Bachelor of Arts in English from the illustrious University of Maryland College Park, as a full-scholarship recipient through the Incentive Awards Program. Afia has conducted community service abroad in Chile, China, and most recently, over 400 hours of volunteer service in Colombia. She was awarded the prestigious Sara Ann Soper Service Award, which recognized her commitment to community service locally and abroad. Afia has held professional work positions at the University of Maryland, Oblon Intellectual Property Firm and Under Armour. She plans to further pursue philanthropic work in the field of Global Relations. She loves servicing Baltimore and she is eager to give back to society at large as often as she can. Afia can be contacted at **afiajyeboah@gmail.com**.

Aisha Watson is a proud Philadelphia native. She attended West Chester University, obtaining a Bachelor's Degree in Special Education. After a few bumps in the road she went on to complete her Master's Degree from Loyola College of Maryland in the area of School Counseling. Ms. Watson is an active member of AMES United Methodist Church in Bel Air MD, where she is a member of the Praise Sign Ministry. Ms. Watson is combining her love of dance and counseling by pursuing her certification in Dance Movement Therapy, and plans to have her own practice after retiring from the Baltimore City Public School System. In addition to serving the Lord, Ms. Watson is a certified aerobics Instructor and can be found teaching Mixxedfit or RIPPED at the local YMCA in Harford County. Ms. Watson is also a Mary Kay Consultant, freelance Make-up Artist and Model. Ms. Watson resides with her 17-year-old son Jamien and their dog, Snickers in Harford County, MD. Contact her at **watsonaisha@hotmail.com**.

Alexus Hobbs is a Baltimore, Maryland native and the oldest of four children. One of her greatest accomplishments is graduating from high school. Not long after finishing high school she received her Associates Degree in Culinary Arts from Stratford University. Alexus's hobbies include writing, reading and sightseeing. She wishes to travel the world finishing and learn more things in the culinary field, so she can one day open her own catering business. She also wants to become a mentor and impacts everyone she encounters. Alexus lives by the idea that hard work and dedication is number one in order to succeed in your goals. Contact her at **alexushobbs@yahoo.com**.

Charon Richardson is a Fashion Designer, Life Design Coach, Speaker, Beauty Curator, Fashion n Style Editor, and Author. She is the founder and Queen Mum of the Queenaration. With Her "Rise and Reign" philosophy, she pours into women around the world the importance of honoring the Queen that lives within them. Her groundbreaking approach of teaching has liberated women to embrace their feminine power and start a journey of self-love. Learn more at **www.queenaration.com**.

Dawania Brown is becoming known throughout the world for her fanatical passion to serve women. She uses her truth and her transparency to share her heart wrenching story of how she conquered domestic violence. She has dedicated her life's work to educating, encouraging and empowering women to activate their God given fortitude so that they, too, can triumph over tragedy. Her passion and power are invigorating and sure to impact change in the lives of many! Dawania's greatest accomplishment is being Mom to her amazing daughters, Tasia and Asia. Contact Dawania at **foxysbaby@gmail.com**.

 Eleshia Thomas

Eleshia Best Thomas is a gifted writer, speaker, mentor, servant of the Lord Jesus Christ, professional childcare provider and co founder of Beauty 4 Ashes outreach ministries in Maryland. Eleshia takes much pride in serving and helping women walk away from their past hurt and embrace their God given purpose through living in their truth, standing on God's word and finding comfort in being the same person in the light as they are in the dark. Eleshia holds a Associate in Arts degree from Baltimore City County College and is currently pursuing a Bachelors degree in Psychology so that she can further serve her community professionally and clinically. Eleshia is a devoted wife and mother of three. She believes by reading and meditating on God's word you will develop an authentic relationship with God, which will transform you into the mature being that he has created you to be. Then you will experience pruning and stretching followed by growth and purpose. Learn more at **www.bit.ly/Beauty4Ashes613** or contact email **Beauty4ashes613@mail.com**.

Joi Hayward

Joi Hayward is a devoted wife, mother, theological student, employee, and member of the Body of Christ. Joi is focused on living a life pleasing to God while serving and supporting her husband and being the best mother to her children. She has accomplished multiple levels of education and is recognized for her exemplary performance in the workplace. Joi believes in the importance of balance and serves as an example to other working wives, mothers, and students. Joi is the founder of God's Confident Woman Ministries. She has hosted three annual conferences in Philadelphia, PA and Columbia, MD. Joi is also the founder of God's Confident Girl, a purity program with two locations; Philadelphia, PA and Columbia, MD. Joi is the author of two books: *Confidence in HIM* and *The Winning Wife*. Joi also contributes word of faith articles worldwide via cfaith.com as a devotion writer. Learn more at **www.GodsConfidentwoman.com**.

Keona Jones

Keona is an educator in an urban public school system. She earned a dual degree in International Business and Management Information Systems from Drexel University and a Masters Degree and an Advanced Professional Certificate in Administration and Supervision from Notre Dame of Maryland in Leadership in Teaching. She is the Executive Director of Queendom T.E.A., a nonprofit dedicated to teaching young ladies how to be queens. While she is committed to be a lifelong learner, her most powerful lessons have come from parenting and traveling the world. Her mission is cultivating cultural connections. Contact her at **Mrs.BaschoGeorge@gmail.com**.

 Lakita Stewart Thompson

Lakita Stewart-Thompson is a servant of the Lord, visionary, mother, mentor, entrepreneur, community advocate, teacher, publisher and #1 best-selling author. She is the Founder/President of the National Association of Mothers & Daughters United Worldwide, Inc., which fosters "Better Bonds Between Daughters and Moms". Her ultimate desire is to have an international one stop resource center for women and girls seeking to overcome life altering circumstances through passion, purpose, partnerships, and philanthropy. Lakita has assisted over 80 women to include young ladies become published authors and share their stories from pain to purpose globally. She is an award winning community service advocate, winning the 2015 SheRose Unsung Organization Award and the 2016 Sisters-In-Law Pillars of Strength Award for her dedication and commitment to making a difference in the lives of women. Her greatest accomplishment and passion in life is the opportunity to mother a 9-year-old young lady named, Destinee. Contact her at **lakitast@icloud.com**.

Mica Saunders is a well known Body Chemist. She is the owner of Breakup2Shapeup. Breakup2Shape is a system that helps women heal from a breakup or divorce using Personal Development and Fitness. In November 2015, Mica was awakened by what I thought was the most devastating news I could ever receive. A phone call from the other woman asking if Mica was the other woman to a man that Mica dedicated a lot of my time and love to for more than 6 years. Mica was completely shocked and devastated. Mica had almost lost myself. After months and months of tears and sharing with friends and family, Mica found a source of relief and determination. I began to turn things around and using my pain to fuel my passion (fitness) and other self love activities. Today, Mica want to help other women who have experienced this same hurt, this same pain, this same feeling of depression and devastation. Visit **Breakup2Shapeup.com** for more.

Mone't S. Horton inspires spirit-led aspiring and current entrepreneurs in fulfilling their life purpose. Ms. Horton, the purpose driven inspirational coach, speaker and psalmist is the Visionary and Chief Inspiration Officer (CIO) of *Mo's Enterprise* LLC which houses *Connecting the Pieces (CTP) Coaching & Consulting Solutions, Mo's Inspiration for You, Leading Ladies Women's Empowerment Network* and *Mo Fashions*. She believes *that all YOU need is within YOU— NOW, is the time to tap in! Mone't helps you move from your REALITY to your WEALTHY PLACE!* Learn more at **www.mos-enterprise.com.**

Shakira Johnson

Shakira Johnson is a Mother, Innovator, Educator and Entrepreneur. Ms. Johnson is a native of Baltimore, Maryland. Currently, she works for Baltimore City Public Schools where she has taught for the past 10 years. In 2007, Ms. Johnson along with a fellow co-worker (Delvrona Hutchins) established the award winning "Inner Harbor East Academy for Young Scholars' Choir". In 2012, Ms. Johnson along with her mom (Cynthia Green) established Kira's Kouture Boutique LLC, a full service mobile Boutique and online store. In 2016, Ms. Johnson and her partner (Knicole Mosby-Taylor) established Women in Business International, an organization for entrepreneurs. Currently, she and her partner (Knicole Mosby-Taylor) facilitate networking events and trainings that empower entrepreneurs and professionals. Learn more at **www.kiraskoutureboutique.com**.

Shawan Pettie

Mentor, professional speaker, etiquette consultant: *Shawan Pettie* is a quiet storm. In 2004, Shawan became a licensed minister, and in 2008 she was ordained as a Deacon at Kingdom Worship Center in Towson, MD, where she currently serves as the Lead Deacon of the church. Dedicated to youth and young adult ministry, Shawan has over 10 years of experience as a Youth and Young Adult leader and has served as a mentor for various non-profit organizations. Because of her passion for excellence, standards and sincere desire to see the family and society restored, she became a Certified Etiquette Consultant at the International School of Protocol. She engages in humanitarian work with the National Alliance for Mental Illness by travelling to speak on the impact of bullying on one's mental and emotional health, and to raise awareness of depression in the African American and Faith-based communities. Contact Shawan at **sepettie@gmail.com**.

Temica Gross is a best-selling author speaker and creative coach. She is affectionately referred to as the Budget Business Boss for her creative knowledge of ways help her clients build and brand their businesses on a budget. A seasoned "Mompreneur", Temica caters her programs, style and approach to meet the needs of new entrepreneur that are balancing life while building their business. She has been featured in several online publications including, The Huffington Post, The Today Show and Madame Noire online. Learn more at **www.TemicaGross.com**.

Violesia Tull is a mother of three beautiful children. She grew up in the inner city of Baltimore. She was sexually abused from the ages of 5 - 14 years old by 7 men, was introduced to pornography at 7 yrs old, idolized the corner life, and held my first gun at 8 years old. Violesia knew her life would be greater. She dropped out of high school during her 12th grade year. She went back to school retrieved her diploma and went on to college. Violesia teaches those who encounter her to get up no matter how many times they fall! Learn more at **www.fashionablychictour.com**.

Please share your photos on social media using the hashtag:

#RepositionedCrowns